MORE PRAISE FOR THE ROAD TO MORI: SMART VILLAGES OF TOMORROW

"UC Berkeley's work on Smart Villages in India led by Professor Solomon Darwin is much needed in today's changing landscape. For over 125 years, GE has met the challenges of industrial change head-on. In today's digital age, robust and well-designed, scalable ecosystems are key catalysts for delivering powerful outcomes to customers. GE Digital is leading this charge by connecting streams of machine data to powerful analytics, providing Industrial companies with valuable insights to manage assets and operations more efficiently. Digital solutions powered by our Predix platform are helping to connect, optimize, and scale applications across a broad range of industries. We're excited by the results of our initiatives that will improve, for example, rural and farming populations that benefit from the emergence of new value-added services and products. The insights laid out in this book complement many of these concepts and initiatives in creating smart villages.

GE Digital's focus on edge computing -- infrastructure that exists close to the sources of data -- is helping to make the Industrial Internet of Things a reality in many places and contexts where this previously wasn't a viable approach. We hope to see this approach enable the formation of ecosystems that serve underserved people in a variety of efficient ways that will broaden participation among companies, governments, and NGOs. Enjoy reading this insightful book."

William Ruh
Chief Executive Officer, GE Digital & Chief Digital Officer, GE

"Solomon Darwin brings a passion and dedication to the Smart Villages program which stems from his personal and professional experiences. Over the last three years that I have been associated with the Smart Villages program, I have been greatly impressed and inspired by the direct impact digital and other innovative technologies have had in transforming the lives of the rural people. As demonstrated in the work done in villages in Andhra Pradesh, this has the potential to bring tangible benefits and visible change in the quality of life of village communities, which comprise 68 percent of India's population. In this book Solomon Darwin reveals how he brings together government, industry and academia on a common platform and incentivizes all three to create scalable, sustainable systems to enable communities to be vested in development and growth, as well as to elevate the 'Happiness Index' in their lives."

Ambassador Venkatesan Ashok
Consul General of India - San Francisco

"The Road to Mori is touching, impactful, and inspirational. I've known Solomon Darwin for several years but never appreciated the mountains he had to climb and the obstacles he faced. He is a role model for the billions of people who live in rural villages or are disenfranchised and left behind. I can't wait to watch the movie!

Solomon Darwin really is the "Father of the Smart Village Movement" and the work he is doing is a wake-up call for anyone who thinks the only future is in the big city."

Vivek Wadhwa
Distinguished Fellow, Carnegie Mellon University
Syndicated Columnist for The Washington Post

"On the Road to Mori proves that Solomon Darwin's vision of the Smart Village can become a reality for the more than 3 billion people living in rural villages all over the world. The Smart Village Movement will dramatically improve their lives and what Darwin calls their "happiness index". It will also, at the same time, enable corporations to find new and exciting markets - rural villages are by far biggest marketplace for innovative products and services. I hope you find Professor Darwin's book as inspiring and thought-provoking -- and in many ways eye-opening -- as I do."

Jim Spohrer, PhD
Director, Cognitive Open Technology, IBM

"Dell EMC is pleased to support the UC Berkeley project for developing new business models for global brands, to participate in untapped rural markets in India. At the core of every new business model is the ability to exploit new technology. Dell Technologies, as the largest provider of essential IT infrastructure technology, is always, interested in how that technology will translate in to real world impacts. We anticipate that large firms will increasingly impact emerging economies across the ecosystem, and our partnerships in research and education with Berkeley will help us understand and influence this trend."

John Roese,
President, Dell-EMC

"Johnson Controls is excited to be a part of the UC Berkeley Smart Villages initiative that brings together the best of todays' digital technologies, platforms and partnerships with other businesses and the government to solve societal challenges to build more safe, sustainable and smarter villages in India." This initiative sets the standard on how businesses, government and knowledge centers like UC Berkeley can work together to solve everyday problems in a self-sustaining manner."

Robert Locke
Senior Vice President, Johnson Controls / Tyco

"UC Berkeley's approach of firms coming together as an ecosystem through an integrated process to deliver value to the farmer is something that has not been tried before. The efforts being made by the university in bringing together large and small firms as an ecosystem to: a) Eliminate costs, b) Facilitate speed to market, c) Increase transparency, d) Lower risk for all e) Increase efficiency in the supply chain f) Time save for all g) Increase yields and revenues h) Enhance data richness i) Promote and Uberization of Assets.

This approach is supported as endorsed personally by our Hon. Chief Minister and we are hoping for great results in the future."
"Our state government in the agricultural sector is committed to be the key facilitator in the whole supply chain process to remove obstacles, bottlenecks and tighten the weakest links in the systems to improve the happiness of the farmer."

Rajsekhar Budithi, IAS
Principle Secretary, Department of Agriculture, Andhra, India

"The time is now for the initiatives of Open Innovation in the Agriculture Ecosystem, and I believe this approach will be welcomed and adopted with great acceptance and appreciation and will set the foundation for a new standard for farming in the future."

Douglas Ry Wagner, PhD
Chief Executive Officer, Agrinos

"World Bank is interested in empowering rural people through digital technology and scalable business models that UC Berkeley brings to the table. The Open Innovation Agriculture and Rural Ecosystem approach developed through Smart Village Program could be scaled up through the institutional investments currently being made in AP. These models are sustainable for economic development of the state in the long term."

Paramesh Shah,
Global Lead for Rural Livelihoods, World Bank, Washington DC

"Wipro is proud to partner with UC Berkeley and the Government of Andhra Pradesh (AP) on an open innovation initiative to develop high impact solutions in the areas of Credit Reputation Management and Citizen Assistance for the rural economy. These solutions leverage next-gen technologies such as Artificial Intelligence, Blockchain, and Machine Learning, amongst others, and will enable the flow of information, micro-capital and ensure increased returns for the rural population of AP. I strongly believe that this partnership will foster an increased collaboration between industry, academia and government to develop solutions that benefit our economy as a whole."

K.R. Sanjiv,
Chief Technology Officer, Wipro

"*Transforming a village through technology starts with empowering the people at the grass roots level in the rural areas. The Smart Village initiative driven through the Berkeley team setup locally in Andhra was a great partnership for the KETOS team to join forces and channel the best of people, talent, technology and resources to result with the right fit for every village and every individual in the new world.*"

Meena Sankaran,
Founder & CEO, Ketos Inc.

"*Agricultural productivity is one of the most basic things that can help the poor to move towards a more prosperous life...I have seen first-hand that agricultural science has enormous potential to increase the yields of small farmers and lift them out of hunger and poverty...Innovations that are guided by smallholder farmers, adapted to local circumstances, and sustainable for the economy and environment will be necessary to ensure food security in the future.*"

Bill Gates

"*The government believes that agricultural growth is only possible by combining advanced technology with effective policies. It is the government's aim to make Andhra the most advanced agricultural state in the country...Villages are the source of wealth.*"

Chief Minister Naidu

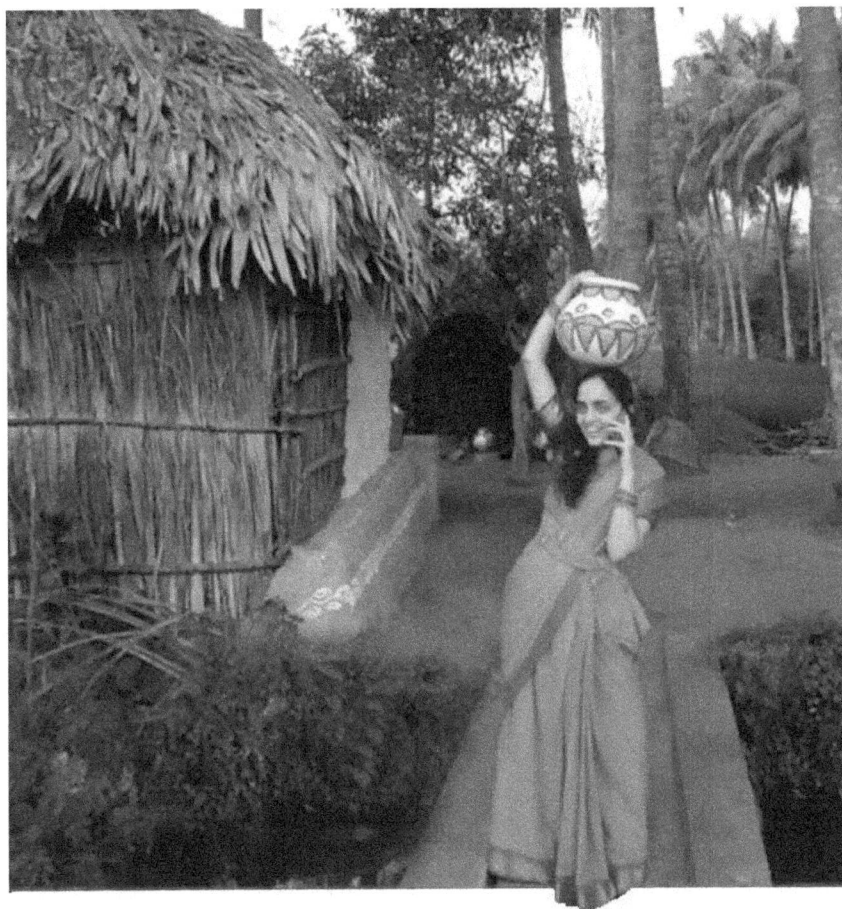

THE ROAD TO MORI

—— SMART VILLAGES OF TOMORROW ——

Solomon Darwin

Peaceful Evolution Publishing

Peaceful Evolution Publishing
Suite 402J
220 Piedmont Avenue
Berkeley, CA 94720
Contact: peacefulevolutionpublishing.com

Ordering Information: Quantity sales. Special discounts are available on quantity purchases by corporations, associations, and others. For details, contact the publisher at the address above. Copies are available in softcover and ebook formats from Amazon and Nook websites.

Printed in the United States of America.

ISBN-13: 978-1732135390
ISBN-10: 1717247946
First Edition

14 13 12 11 10 / 10 9 8 7 6 5 4 3 2 1

Developmental Editor: David Grebow
Associate Editor: Jon Zilber
Cover Photograph Model: Evani Shreya
Cover Design: Jessica David
Illustrations: Sibghatmirza

This book is dedicated to the 3.4 billion rural people currently deprived of access to global markets due to lack of connectivity, information, resources, training, and tools for the digital era, with hope for a future in which they can thrive.

Table of Contents

Foreword

*By Professor Henry Chesbrough, the Father of Open Innovation
UC Berkeley Haas School of Business.*

The alleviation of rural poverty is one of the defining challenges of our time. It is directly connected to several of the Sustainability Development Goals of the United Nations and promises to unleash new sources of growth for participants in the global economy. This book will take you on a new journey to this important destination.

It has been an inspiration 'to watch the Smart Villages initiative unfold over the past three years. The seed of this idea originated with a man who was originally from Mori village in the state of Andhra Pradesh. Through the tireless efforts of his family, Solomon Darwin made his way to the U.S. Many years later, after a distinguished career in accounting and corporate finance, this now-educated man encountered the concept of open innovation.

It was a fortuitous meeting, for it catalyzed the transformation of Professor Darwin's thinking, and provided a powerful concept to unlock a new approach to rural development. Earlier approaches to rural development were predicated on the idea of market failure: there wasn't enough income in rural areas to attract companies and markets to engage with them, beyond the rudiments of subsistence agriculture. The only remedy was government support, in the form of aid and loans, in hopes of helping desperately poor people improve their lives. To do anything, one must do everything.

1

After decades of government-led development assistance, though, there hasn't been enough benefit for enough people to overcome the trap of rural poverty. And the assistance doesn't scale. When the government aid ends, the benefit stops. A new approach is needed, to break the cycle of rural poverty, empower individuals to grow their skills, access markets, overcome corruption, and scale beyond the initial area where assistance was received.

Open innovation is based on the concept of harnessing knowledge flowing from the outside in one's innovation processes and allowing unused knowledge to flow outside for others to use in their innovations. In other words, one doesn't have to do everything on one's own. One can harness the knowledge and skills of others in the process of innovation.

The companies participating in the Smart Villages initiative are employing Open Innovation to innovate new products and services for the bottom of the pyramid. Mori village is an ideal testbed for these companies to use in their explorations. These villagers have many needs and few resources. The needs of villagers and their willingness to pay to address those needs are difficult to understand for those who live, work, and think far away from the village. One needs to investigate these villagers' needs and experiment with alternative business models that provide real value to the villager, at a price they are able and willing to pay.

However, the villagers in Mori village are not terribly different from villagers in many other rural villages in Andhra Pradesh. Therefore, the discoveries that companies make in serving the needs of Mori villagers will likely be quite useful in serving the needs of other villages as well. This can open the rural world for these innovative companies, allowing them to serve a large and rapidly growing market. This is an attractive prize for these companies, making these experiments in Mori village well worth taking.

The pilot stage of the Smart Villages project succeeded in attracting more than 40 companies and organizations to Mori village. These companies are not providing charity, however. They are making small business development investments to learn about the needs of rural villagers for products and services they might choose to provide. Importantly, these investments will reveal what villagers value enough to pay for it directly with their funds. This is a kind of business model discovery that we see in Lean Startup approaches to business model innovation, albeit in a very different context.

There is a further ecosystem effect that is emerging in the Smart Villages project. The presence of one company in the village makes it more attractive for subsequent companies to also locate a person in the village. The result is a vibrant ecosystem of possible products and services for local villagers. Note that no single company or organization could martial all these disparate resources on their own. It takes an ecosystem of organizations, all seeking to understand villagers' needs and their willingness to pay, to obtain this open innovation ecosystem.

In this way, open innovation can stimulate the emergence of Smart Villages, empower villagers to break the cycle of rural poverty that traps billions of people today and creates new market opportunities for enterprising companies willing to devote their time (and a small amount of resources) to experiment in these settings.

At the same time, Professor Darwin is innovating the concept of open innovation itself. Open innovation began as an explanation of innovation for "high-tech" organizations in the developed world. Through this book, we see how the idea can be applied successfully in completely different circumstances. I congratulate him on this achievement and look forward to its further progress as we watch the Smart Villages Movement take hold around the world.

Preface

This book is a roadmap that will show you how to get to the Smart Villages of tomorrow. These communities are empowered by digital technologies and platforms that support open innovation. They have always-on access to global markets. They also represent the best opportunity to use a proven business model to develop low-margin high volume products and services needed by more than 3.4 billion people living and working in villages around the world. These Smart Villages will become the primary source of innovation for your business as information and knowledge flow in and out through these open innovation platforms. If you are looking for new markets, *The Road to Mori: Smart Villages of Tomorrow* is your doorway into this future.

There has been a great deal of work performed in recent years exploring the design, development and deployment of Smart Cities, urban areas whose resources and people are all connected by digital technology. This work enables these cities to become "smarter" and use city resources more efficiently and sustainably. Even the smartest cities have limits. Size can transform the initial economies of scale into dis-economies when the city grows taller, compresses further and reaches its outer limits of growth. The smart technology used today to manage and harmonize a city infrastructure is complicated and expensive and, as the technology inevitably changes and improves, it becomes increasingly difficult for the city to keep up, retool and retrofit that infrastructure continually.

Even the smartest city continues to have the problem of neighborhoods that never become communities, and neighbors who never communicate with one another. Many of the issues consistently plaguing urban areas remain even after they become "smart" – crime, homelessness, demand for more services and increasing stress. Their impact on the environment is unfavorable since cities develop less haphazardly and organically, rendering them unable to function as stewards of the environment.

On the other hand, the problems of urban areas are not a significant part of the daily life of the smaller rural communities that are more manageable. The village is a better candidate for forming cooperative ecosystems, living in harmony with the natural environment, nurturing the valuable arable agricultural land and fresh water. The communities are places in which people are more connected to one another, to their environment, with a higher score on the happiness index and pride of place not often seen in the city.

In India, and other countries in which villages are the predominant way of life, the smaller, more close-knit communities are more easily adaptable and agile in their use of mobile and affordable digital technologies. Villages represent emerging economies in which necessity breeds frugal innovation, created in an environment of limited resources driven by unlimited imagination. The term "Reverse Innovation" refers broadly to the process whereby goods developed as inexpensive models to meet the needs of the developing countries, are then repackaged as innovative low-cost goods for Western more developed nations. Increasingly Villages will become the primary source of innovation for business ecosystems as information and knowledge flow in and out through open innovation platforms.

With 67% of India's population (and almost half of the world's people) choosing to live in villages, they need a way to make their villages "smart." It is important to note that a Smart Village is an idea and not any specific place. A Smart Village is a community empowered by digital technologies and open innovation platforms to access global markets. These villages are a means of empowering people with access to tools, resources, real-time transparent information, and uninterrupted internet connectivity.

The site of the first of many Smart Villages is Mori in the State of Andhra Pradesh, India. The project, led by Solomon Darwin, is a collaboration between the Garwood Center, University of California, Berkeley and the Andhra Pradesh Government. The vision is to increase how satisfied and happy people feel across rural Andhra Pradesh by implementing digital technologies to solve various problems. These digital technologies come from 22 global corporate partners who work with the villagers to identify their challenges and tailor their innovations to meet their needs. The project is the first to employ Open Innovation approaches and processes based on research work done at the Garwood Center. Mori became a Co-innovation Lab and an area in the village was set-up where villagers in Mori engage with the companies to create prototypes of products and services that can be used by the villagers for further scaling everywhere.

The goal is to use the Open Innovation and Business Model approach to bring Mori into a more significant ecosystem, using digital technology and access to global markets, in a way that is scalable to neighboring villages and ultimately the whole country. It is the road that villages can take to move from the relative isolation and obscurity of the 19th-century industrial economy and enter the modern 21st-century marketplace of the knowledge economy with access to products and services, knowledge and know-how. It is the only way to create a genuinely sustainable future and improve the standard and living and happiness index of the 3.4 billion people living in these rural communities.

Mori has shown that the villagers have a strong desire to embrace digital technology to access global markets. This desire was coupled with the readiness of global brands to invest in this enormous untapped market. That was demonstrated on a warm Thursday, December 29, 2016, in Mori when over forty thousand villagers from India, and eighty corporate executives from around the world, came together to celebrate this new idea of a Smart Village Movement. The Mori project has successfully produced a variety of prototypes. Every home in Mori today has optical fiber connections. The initial plans include telemedicine, education, skill development and, entrepreneurship. These programs include smart technology for agriculture for rice farmers, bicycles for 50 Asha healthcare workers for home visits, coupled with the first healthcare records to be stored in the cloud. There is also a program helping shrimp farmer, weavers and, solar system entrepreneurs gain access to the knowledge and global markets they need to be successful.

The goal is to be able to scale the models developed in Mori to the others 650,000 villages in India. But that is not the end of the road. Ultimately, Solomon Darwin's dream of a Smart Village in Mori

10

becomes The Smart Village Movement for villages around the world. The goal of the movement is not to help the poor but to end poverty by creating entrepreneurs and jobs. This goal is achieved by large firms creating business models and ecosystems that are scalable and sustainable.

The story of this movement begins on the road to Mori.

Chapter One: In the Beginning

"The soul of India lives in its villages." M.K. Gandhi

The Road to Mori: Smart Villages of Tomorrow is the path that I took to arrive at the vision of the Smart Village Movement™. It is my story, of a young boy born into poverty as an untouchable in India, who comes to America where a focus on learning and education, perseverance, and persistence, lead to great business success. It is my journey through years of outstanding academic scholarship to learn the ideas that formed the concept of the Smart Village. More than anything, it is the path I took to return and help the villagers of Mori improve their standard of living and increase their level of happiness. Mori is now the forerunner on the road to the Smart Village Movement around the world.

My thoughts and words are in this record of what began as a project in the village of Mori, India and is destined to become the Smart Village Movement for rural populations everywhere.

I believe that business models should be built on the digital technologies of the future for villages be become smart. Only then they can leapfrog to transform their rural landscape. One such breakthrough technology I helped to bring to Andhra Pradesh is Free Space Optical

Communication (FSOC) technology that was tested and piloted in the Mori Village. In the fall of 2016, I made several presentations to Google X's senior management convincing them to pilot that technology in Mori in Andhra Pradesh and participate in the UC Berkeley's Smart Village Project. I made a compelling case and convinced Google's management to test the technology where it is most needed, and where scalable business models could be developed. FSOC links deliver high-speed, high-capacity connectivity over long distances using beams of light which is similar to how data is transmitted through fiber optic cables using light, but unlike traditional fiber optic. This eliminates the need to dig trenches or string cable along the poles. The FSOC innovation saves huge amount of capital expenditure and ongoing maintenance while delivering a high-quality signal, saving time for all stakeholder within the ecosystem. What is even more valuable to businesses is the efficient communication system promotes speed to market in the delivery of their products and services.

A year following the pilot and showcasing it to the Chief Minister in Mori, it became a reality. On December 15, 2017, The Economic Times of India reported that the Andhra Pradesh government signed agreements with Alphabet X, the moonshot factory of Alphabet (earlier known as Google X) for a Fibergrid project. The government of Andhra Pradesh has agreed to bring this breakthrough Free Space Optical Communication (FSOC) technology to Mori to provide internet access through the government Fiber Grid Project. And on January 25, 2018, FSOC was showcased during the World Economic Forum at Davos by Chief Minister Naidu.

The Smart Village project witnessed tremendous participation from national and international corporations; over 80 corporations aligned with our vision of sustainable scaling and development. Thirty-seven excellent examples of Open Innovation and Co-Innovation were realized during our phase-One. As a result, most of our corporate partners extended their participation in Phase Two, with 95 - 100 companies participating. A good number of corporations are succeeding in their efforts.

However, there have been several solutions that did not fit in a rural setting or meet corporate objectives of individual firms, and as a result they dropped out over the course of time. A few of them are facing internal problems and road blocks but are continuing to participate with our help to overcome these challenges. We are using open innovation approaches to find possible solutions to overcome the barriers, road blocks, and tighten the weakest links. We were able to apply new knowledge and perspectives for Phase Two. Several new solutions were added during this phase as we were exploring more issues and pain points of our villagers. As some companies had to leave, new companies joined our movement with new sources and innovations to solve problems and plug into the Smart Village ecosystem.

Unlike any other study on this subject, our research on the ground has been very rigorous based on one-to-one interaction with villagers to develop models from bottom-up taken the reality on the ground into account. One Harvard case, through the California Management Review, Berkeley, on the Mori Smart Village project[1] was already published, and second Harvard case will be released in May 2018 The second Harvard case study will be based on numerous surveys performed by the Berkeley trained Smart Village Team in India. Both cases discuss the urgent need for global brands to engage the rural populations to expand markets.

A white paper was prepared and submitted to Bill Gates on "Smart Village Ecosystems: An Open Innovation Approach"[2] on November 10, 210 during visit to India. The paper discussed our ecosystem approach of integrated process of delivering value to the farmer which has not been tried before. The study was based on over 20 UC Berkeley Corporate partners and one-on-one field surveys with over 10,000 farmers in Andhra Pradesh. The effort being made by the university in bringing together large and small firms as an ecosystem to:

- eliminate costs
- increase speed to market
- increase transparency
- reduce risk for stakeholders
- increase efficiency in the supply chain
- time save for all
- increase yields and revenues.

All this is possible by removing bottlenecks and tightening the weakest link in the supply chain.

This book offers many learnings from operating in the field during the past two years. We plan to put them to use as we refine our models to attract corporate investment in rural economies, while empowering

16

people with digital technologies that will provide access to global markets and sources of knowledge. It is the futuristic technologies like FSOC from corporations like Alphabet X that will rapidly move the Smart Village Movement forward.

Our learnings and the knowledge of the on-ground experiences were captured in our manual on "Road to Smart Villages" that was developed over the course of two years. Our motive behind launching the manual is to share the expertise developed by the Smart Village team in order to replicate the Smart Village model to other states in India and across the world. The "Road to Smart Villages: An Open Innovation Approach"[3] beautifully captures the processes, approaches, strategies, techniques, failures, successes and learnings in developing various successful and unsuccessful models throughout the project. The manual will be used by the Smart Village Team as their guide as others follow the road to a Smart Village. It is a work-in-progress, an evolving knowledge repository for building Smart Villages.

Chapter Two: The Inevitability of Change

When I was a little boy growing up in Mori Village, the village had one transistor pocket size radio made by Sony that someone from Dubai brought while returning home. The whole village shared this one transistor every evening. The crowds gathered during evening times after a hard day's work in the field to listen to the news and music coming out of this little box. So that everyone can hear, it was put up on a large brick pile in the center of the village. One evening we all stayed up until midnight to listen to the voice of Neil Armstrong from the moon. It was not too long after that everyone had one as Sony made it affordable.

AT&T won the Nobel Prize for the discovery of the Transistor in 1948. The closed innovation policy at AT&T robbed my village and the people of the world of the joy of music, information and knowledge flow for over ten years. It was Sony, an unknown company at the time that came out of the ashes of World War 11, that shipped out the most affordable and portable transistor in 1958. The same thing happened when Nokia introduced an affordable cell phone following Motorola's very expensive Razor that had so many features that were irrelevant to the people in India. Today, in the village of Mori, everyone, even sweeper and scavenger who are the lowest members of society has an affordable cell phone.

Last summer, I was in Mori and one day as I was finishing up my breakfast, I let my kitchen worker know that I am on my way to the bank to do some transactions. Upon hearing this she told me not to waste my time and use my cell phone instead. She said, "let me show you this app as I transfer money to my daughter and move funds between accounts all the time". I was amazed that my house maid who did not even finish primary school was teaching me, a professor who teaches innovation at Berkeley about the benefits of digital technology.

Change is inevitable; it happens at a different speed depending on where you live. The myth is that rural, isolated villages slowly change and that the almost plodding daily struggle is simply their way of life. The truth is that the people in rural villages everywhere are already creatively using the digital technology to transform their lives. Smartphones, computers, the internet and more are being employed every day. Smart Villages, as I came to define them, are an opportunity to focus and accelerate the energy and inventiveness already changing these rural communities. It offers global corporations a new open innovation approaches to business models in which the enormous number of Smart Villages around the world will provide new markets for products and services. Smart Village products and services that will improve the community's standard of living, increase their level of satisfaction. And raise the score on the happiness index.

Villages like Mori, in the State of Andhra Pradesh, are often perceived as places that the modern technology-driven world has not yet touched. A slow-paced rural place for farming, fishing, trading, and small businesses, built around a town square or central plaza, where people recognize and greet you by name, and know your family history by heart. A timeless place, where the speed and compression of the city have been avoided, along with all the easily available technology that drives the urban style of living. Appearances are deceiving. Living conditions in the village, without the most basic services, make life difficult and dangerous. Even without modern digital technology, the answer to a better life is to innovate, and there are many examples.

In the State of Madhya Pradesh, the light weight of the tractors made plowing the fields even harder. Tractor salespeople were more than eager to sell expensive weights to make the tractor plow more easily. The farmer's answer was water. Fill the tires with water and they tractors were heavier for zero cost. The innovation has helped millions of farmers across the sub-continent.[4]

India is the second largest producer of cotton in the world. Cotton is also one of the most difficult and back-breaking crops to harvest. Nattubhai Vader new two things. It was incredibly hard work and finding villagers to pick the cotton was becoming harder and harder. Out of necessity, he invented the cotton harvester, a large vacuum with spinning rubber hoses attached to the back of a tractor. In one hour his harvester picks as much cotton as ten people could pick in two days.[5]

Today, villagers live in what Marshall McLuhan called a "Global Village"[6], connected to the rest of the world by digital technology, from smartphones to the internet. In this Global Village, change is inevitable and is happening faster than ever as each village becomes a node in a global network connected to other villages, sharing what they are innovating and learning. What the villagers are doing may not change, but how they are doing it will be different. As a result, the villages in this new world will become smarter.

The goal is to employ the innovative spirit of the villagers and provides them access to digital tools, resources, real-time information, and uninterrupted internet connectivity. The result is a community empowered by digital technologies and open innovation platforms to access global markets. This is not only the story of transformation of a village into a Smart Village, but it is also the story of my return to Mori, the village where I was born, to help people realize of what a Smart Village can do for villages all over India and the world.

Chapter Three: The Return to Mori

I arrived on American soil on September 13, 1971, in San Francisco, brought here by my father along with my family. I did not want to leave India as I knew that I could not cope with the challenges this advanced civilization would bring into my life. I was unprepared, unqualified, and suffered from very low self-esteem due to growing up in a segregated village as an Untouchable. I had just turned seventeen, and my level of education was at a fifth-grade level at best. I could only barely read and write English, and I did not know other subjects beyond that. It was my poor education in a village school, where I was not taught much for many years, that got me dismissed from the formal school system while I was in fifth grade after moving from the Mori to a city Visakhapatnam before arriving here. It was demoralizing to be the oldest boy sitting in a city school from a remote village. The fact that I could not make the minimum marks to pass the grade added to my stress. This consistent failure very early in my life due to the lack of self-worth had me thinking to end my life and resulted in one failed suicide attempt.

However, upon coming to America and having access to the many opportunities regardless of my caste, limited education and the many handicaps, I could rise above them. What got me back to Mori is the realization that many in my village and many others like it can rise above their circumstances and succeed. Today through digital technologies and death of time and distance, the access that I have here to the resources, tools, information, and opportunities, could be provided in Mori, and 650,000 villages like it. Yes, access to Equal

Opportunities is a Great Equalizer especially for a poor boy from an untouchable caste like me. You can find more details about my incredible journey in my forthcoming book, "The Untouchables." with a preview at the end of this book.

How was Mori chosen as the place to model what a Smart Village can accomplish? I began my life in Mori as an untouchable. It is a way of life that most people would run from and never return. The arc of my life, from my birth and family, to America with my father, through a variety of senior executive corporate jobs in the business world, to finally a prestigious position in a well-respected academic institution is the backbone of this story. It takes a fantastic turn when I drew on all my experience and learning and had a vision of the Smart Village, a rural community driven by powerful business models that can transform the villages of India. Help them solve their pain points and become thriving hubs of innovation and development for products and services that will improve their lives and increase their happiness. I believed my approach would rapidly transform the villages into Smart Villages, communities empowered by digital technologies and open innovation platforms to access global markets. A place where people stay and even return after they tried living in an urban community. I needed a place to start, a prototype that would prove it would work. Born an untouchable, shunned by the society, the village I chose to return is Mori. This is the story of my journey and the birth of the Smart Village Movement.

My life began in Mori, a small village in the State of Andhra Pradesh. Back then my village was a clean and peaceful place with many hardworking people who labored in the fields. Eight thousand people, located in southern India between the Bay of Bengal and the mouth of the Godavari, one of the many rivers that flow into the Indian Ocean. It was a village like many other villages in India, lost in a time warp, unchanged for hundreds of years despite the changes that have happened in the outside world.

I left this village as a teenager to the United States along with my father who made his way here under the most improbable circumstances.

I returned many times over the years since I left to find that there was little to no improvements. In many ways, things had gotten worse. The canals that I once swam in and fished are full of pollutants and plastic waste along with animal and human excretions. The roads are more crowded with autos and buses with a lot of noise and pollution. Despite the number of schools that have come up, including the Riverside School I started, there is a high level of youth unemployment. Year after year many farmers stopped growing their crops as costs exceeded revenues, and as a result suicides among them have gone steadily up as they could not repay their debts.

It was ironic to me that there had been so many new advances in technology, business model innovations and exponential growth in information and knowledge since I left my village as a teen. All this progress did not offer much benefit to the rural populations where most of the people in the world live.

High levels of corruption and lack of transparency at all levels seemed to be bottlenecks and the weakest links in the system, stopping people who are willing to improve themselves.

The farmer who is processing cashews in the village wanted to know how he could package them and put them on the internet to make it available to the world. He is looking for simple straightforward answers. He wants to know how he could register a business and get a license to export – whom to partner with and how to lower his cost to create value to the end consumer in the US. There were no easy answers for him to find.

A lady in the village who earns only $10.00 a saree that takes many weeks to weave on her vintage handloom machine wanted to know how she could put her inventory on the internet – she is tired of earning the government set price for her saree that takes her a month to weave. Many of my friends in America feel $100 is a steal for a beautiful and brightly-colored hand-woven Chirala cotton or Madhavaram silk saree with designs made by the Mori weavers. She needs information, tools and access to markets to do this. Information, tools and platforms that many people in the world use every day are not available to her.

It is this kind of education, connection and access to information that is most needed in the 650,000 villages in India to bring about greater happiness, health, and opportunity, to bring the villages into the 21st century.

I imagined a different kind of village, one in which people could communicate easily and cooperate with each other. A village that would work best when it is a community of people looking out for one another and realizing that as each one succeeds the entire village succeeds. A place where the basic needs for healthcare, education, and opportunity met sustainably. Where the voices of the people decided the best direction to take, and they helped choose the best products and services to provide the most value to the village. Most importantly, a village that was connected to the outside world using the digital technology, the same technology that was commonly used in most of the urban centers in the world. In other words, I began to imagine the outlines of what life in Mori could be like as a Smart Village.

The Road to Mori as a Smart Village began December 2015 with a request from Chief Minister Naidu of Andhra Pradesh. I led a project that year with my students at Berkeley on Smart Cities in India. Minister Naidu invited me to do a similar project on how to make villages smart. He wanted to know what technologies would be employed and how business models would attract global brands to rural markets.

During that meeting, the value proposition to the government was reviewed:

- Potential investment from Silicon Valley firms and Start-ups
- Benefit from the research conducted by us to formulate their innovation policy
- Encouraging entrepreneurship in villages – creating jobs
- Meeting the needs of the villagers to improve their level of satisfaction and happiness
- Benefit from the user manual created by Garwood Center in the process followed for pilots.

What follows is a summary of Berkeley's involvement leading the successful prototype Smart Village project in India. It is an indication of how the Smart Village idea can spread across the world and be used by villages everywhere.

The Smart Village project in Mori, India was designed and managed in three phases:

Phase One

Phase One of the research project was started in June of 2016 and was concluded on December 29, 2016. This initial phase of the Smart Village Project consisted of taking one typical village – Mori as a laboratory to develop frameworks and test various digital technologies and business models that could empower rural people.

The primary objective was to test the following on ground:

- The readiness of rural people to adopt digital technologies,
- The willingness of large firms to invest in villages to generate money through scaling,
- Adaptability of large firms to adopt new business models,
- Adaptability and the bandwidth of the government to incorporate these technologies.
- The above required training and capacity building of the Smart Village workforce, as well as designing and setting up surveys, processes, and procedures to do the following:
- Identify: Pain Points, Pain Relievers, and Pain Relieving Agents (Large Firms & Startups)

- Ideate: What Business Models work? What Ecosystems need to be created?
- Co-Innovate: Pivot the technologies and models, then engage villagers for feedback
- Implement & Scale: Not done - Phase 2 was needed to test Phase 1 more broadly.

In Phase One, over 8,000 villagers in Mori (95% of the people) were invited, and everyone attended the Co-Innovation Lab to engage with the teams during three different intervals over a six-month period.

Major Silicon Valley firms were invited to participate in the project, and many responded by spending their time, resources and money over a six-month period. Over 22 large firms participated, as well as a few startups. Over 80 corporate executives flew into Mori to present their technologies to the Chief Minister.

Garwood published our first case study on Smart Villages where the Chief Minister was the protagonist. CMR California Management Review published the case that was distributed through the Harvard Case Study program. The case was submitted to the Chief Minister and his cabinet for review. The Chief Minister realized upon completion of Phase One that his villagers are ready for technology, and many global brands were ready to explore and invest in his state.

Phase Two

The Chief Minister of Andhra was greatly pleased with the results and signed a Memorandum of Understanding with UC Berkeley. He commissioned 472 villages to be a part of the Smart Village project that represented the diversity of his villages.

The Smart Village Project Phase 2 offered large firms and startups an opportunity to develop and test "Scalable Business Models" to generate new sources of revenue.

The value proposition we offered to potential contributing corporations included the following:

- Access to an efficient structure established by Garwood to test their offerings in the villages by our teams that were organized by districts, counties, and villages.
- The core team of eight would be like a start-up and live together in Mori. The 34 county directors from the districts and about 500 village interns would be recruited.
- The directors and interns would live in the villages they were from. The interns would do surveys, collect data and provide feedback to firms to re-pivot their offerings.
- Business model canvas and lean start-up methods would be employed to fine-tune the companies' business models and adapt their technologies to address the villager's pain points.
- Develop business models for technology offerings that can scale in India's untapped market where approximately 65% of India's Population live.
- Receive input from Garwood Center's faculty to formulate scalable business models based on data and feedback collected on the ground.

- Information about government programs that enable or deter innovation and growth of foreign firms were also being studied.
- Co-Innovation process with participating firms to form collaborations and partnerships to enhance their offerings is also being observed during the process.
- Build social capital with a local ecosystem of universities, government entities, and enterprises.

Our trained and experienced Smart Village Team to use Open Innovation to Co-Innovate through direct dialogue with villagers in 472 villages (from May 2017- May 2018). The objective is to understand how the right business models and digital technologies can empower the villagers to make money and in turn provide a way for the global brands to prosper in India's rural villages.

The Phase Two results and technologies were showcased to Bill Gates during his trip to India in November 2017. A white paper was published and was presented to him and his foundation.

Phase Three

With the successful completion of Phase Two, Phase Three will start, if the government chooses to scale the Smart Village models developed by the team in 36,000 villages throughout Andhra Pradesh.

I returned to my village in 2016 to begin the transformation I imagined was possible, and help transform my birthplace, to be a shining example for villages in India and everywhere.

For more details, see Appendix 1: The introduction to The Road to Smart Villages: An Open Innovation Approach.

Chapter Four: The Pain Points

If a single transistor radio could bring so much joy to my village, what might result if we consciously and systematically designed small innovations intended to be scalable, have high impact, and act as catalysts for positive change? If a cell phone in the hands of one villager, like my house maid, who can save couple of hours by avoiding going to a bank, just multiply hours saved by 3.4 billion people living in villages around the world.

Some people may feel that society is static. They believe that human nature is constant, and human nature dictates how we live our lives. But the only thing that remains constant in our society is the reality of constant change. Throughout human history, we've seen radical transformations triggered by small sparks that changed everything in an instant. The industrial revolution. The invention of elevators that made skyscrapers possible which, in turn, made dense cities economically viable. The Internet. Even tin cans for storing food.

Before I began exploring ways to trigger transformations in the millions of villages around the globe, I had been teaching courses at Berkeley in building Smart Cities and how that could transform the world. The idea was that by building such cities in the developing world, these areas could leapfrog over decades of social evolution. These cities would create an infrastructure that would not merely be a vast improvement over their status, but would also place them, in many ways, ahead of cities in the developed world. These older cities, built centuries ago were now suffering from crumbling infrastructure, such as the subways under Manhattan, or the catacombs of Paris, that can't quickly be updated. For a variety of reasons -- ranging from rampant corruption to political inertia -- the vision of the Smart City in the developing world languished.

But what I realized from that exploration was that villages didn't need massive shiny new expensive infrastructure. We do not need to destroy the old or retrofit the existing structures but start fresh and leapfrog into the digital era. Something as simple as a single transistor radio could provide an entire village with joy. What specific modest steps could transform these villages not into ultra-modern cities, but into more sustainable and fulfilling villages -- Smart Villages as we call them.

After several years of research, testing, and analysis, the Smart Villages concept -- and the changes it will bring -- are far from impossible. And the Smart Village Movement is not merely possible -- it is inevitable.

This is the story of what Smart Villages are, how I believe they will emerge and evolve, the impact they can have on the 3.4 billion people who live in the world's villages, and the companies and entrepreneurs that will find new opportunities in the Smart Village market.

The Smart Village is a solution to the many problems defined by the people who live and work there. Their "pain points" included the challenges the farmers face by not being connected to knowledge and know-how about pesticides and fertilizers. The difficulty weavers encounter not having access to broader markets. And the pain a mother feels when her daughter cannot find immediate help when she is sick. All these and more are the pain points that I heard, really heard and decided to change. How do you hear `so many pain points and structure a solution that can encompass all of them? The answer to that challenge was the ideas I had begun to realize in the Smart Village.

It started by realizing the villagers desperately needed to take advantage of existing, yet affordable, digital technology. After empowering the community with digital technologies – smartphones, laptops, and uninterrupted internet connectivity – the next key step would be to add open innovation platforms that enabled the villages to co-create products and services with global partners. Partners who were motivated to help because they saw the potential of this enormous new market. Add in access to marketplaces anytime and anyplace for their produce and goods, and a sustainable solution to many of the pain points began to appear. This was the way the idea, different from other approaches, started to take shape in my mind. The big question remaining was simple: Would it work?

I recalled hearing people talk about their pain points, about how difficult life was in Mori. Everything I heard kept pointing to the solution I imagined in the Smart Village.

Farmers often complained that the middlemen in the distribution chain took far too much for the service they provide. The farmers were left with too little ever to get ahead. And there were always loses in the rice crop because of too little information about soil conditions, use, and supplies of fertilizers and pesticides. Even getting up-to-date weather forecasts was hard without good communications. Because most of the farmers leased their land, it was almost impossible to get out from under when they earned so little and had their hard work pay off for themselves.

Then there were conversations that I will never forget. A rice farmer once told me about the way his crop failed because he did not know what other rice farmers had learned.

"My crop last year was terrible. Not enough water. I could not rely on the weather news always a day late. I was planting the rice saplings as I always did, and they need a lot of water." I knew there was information about new ways of farming, an approach that used a direct seed method, placing the seeds directly into the rice paddy, so the seeds needed much less water. I had also heard that farmers in a nearby state are using laser lights to make sure the fields are flat. Flatter fields keep the water in the longer without it flowing to the downhill sides. All this valuable information was unavailable to him.

Mori's 8,000 residents are spread across the village's 1,316 acres. Many of them work in the rice, avocado, coconut, and textiles industries. Others process cashews or farm shrimp or mangoes. Cashew processing is done in homes and offers decent margins but is dangerous done the traditional way and is a source of carbon emissions because of the high heat required during the processing.

Life in the village presents residents with constant challenges, including lack of access to basic resources such as health care, sanitation, clean water, and power. The power is on for only 20 hours in the winter and 12 in the summer. There were approximately 800 total toilets in the village, leading to open defecation, which leads to active mosquito breeding. In turn, the mosquitoes spread malaria and dengue, a virus that is a leading cause of illness and death in the tropics and subtropics and for which there are not yet any vaccines to prevent infection. Drinking water is barely adequate, and the water I drank from the tap was hard and salty. I often saw women walking along carrying heavy water pots on their heads on the way back to their homes.

Public healthcare access in the village is limited and, for many villagers, seeing a private doctor is much too expensive. One Mori resident described the situation to me when she said, "Healthcare is expensive. Since we are uneducated, we cannot question what the local village doctor says. Several people in villages like ours choose to approach godmen or spiritual healers to cure their ailments. I have heard of cases where people's health has gone downhill due to improper diagnosis, poor care, and lack of proper healthcare facilities." Although Mori does have a small public clinic, the nearest hospital is 25 kilometers away from the village. Only two doctors are servicing the entire village. Limited access to care is not unique to Mori. In fact, 80 percent of healthcare providers in India are in or near urban centers.

I heard from one physician who told me, "There is an urgent need for doctors, yet very few are willing to work here. My family is still living in the city. They are unable to settle here due to a lack of basic education, healthcare, and sanitation facilities. My income here is also meager in comparison to what I would have gotten by working in city hospitals or as a private medical practitioner." Additional doctors are not able to work in the village because they cannot support their families. There are registered medical practitioners who do the best they can, too often simply prescribing antibiotics and other shots to cure their patients.

We never think about it in the city, but livestock, including buffaloes and chickens, play an important role in the economy of the village, and the health of the livestock was a problem. Many farmers in Mori depend on their buffaloes for milk, meat, dung, and hides. Chickens provide eggs and meat. The Buffaloes are also a major source of power helping farmers plow fields and pull wagons and carts. I saw many more bullock-driven carts than cars. There were no veterinary doctors in the village, and sick livestock, especially buffaloes, resulted in a loss of revenue.

Access to education is also limited, with too few places in the two government-run public schools for all the village's children. Even in those grades, there are not very many trained, qualified teachers. There is no instruction for children in grades one through five conducted in English. Feeding students in these schools is problematic with the midday meals poorly scheduled and offered. The few private schools in the area are too expensive for most villagers to attend.

Young adults who wish to pursue careers in medicine, engineering, the law, or education must be able to speak English to enter professional education programs. Students must travel 6-12 miles to attend grades above level five. Even when they can get into those higher education schools, bus transportation is often erratic, making it difficult for students to get to school on time.

The lack of good economic opportunities also presents villagers with challenges. I often heard the situation summed up by the story one villager described me. "I used to work as a daily wage worker in gruesome conditions at a textile mill where working full-time, I earned 30 rupees [approximately 45 U.S. cents] a day. Now even that work is gone." Typical wages in Mori are about 180 rupees to 250 rupees per day, about \$2.65 to about \$3.69. Lack of access to information means the workforce has no awareness about any choices.

There is another important pain point I heard. The lack of tools and resources means people struggle to find ways to prosper. There is a dire need for and demand for higher wages of 450 rupees per day (approximately \$6.70) rather than 180 to 250 rupees per day (approximately \$2.65 to about \$3.70). All that was needed was access to a market. To make matters even worse, government work programs with the best intentions add to the labor shortage. These programs provide short-term solutions to the problems by paying for work on temporary projects that the villagers become dependent upon. After the project is over, the work goes away. What's needed is something long-term, a sustainable solution.

Furthermore, mechanization and automation have destroyed many jobs in the handloom, pottery, handicraft, and goldsmith industries. For those people still employed in the vintage made-by-hand weaving industry, wages are low, and unsold inventory is continually mounting. Recently unsold handloom inventory was worth between

3,000,000 and 5,000,000 rupees (about $44,900 to $74,800). Beautiful vintage sarees made in Mori without a marketplace in which to be sold.

Plus, their trades were vanishing as better paying jobs became more attractive to the people who might have chosen to become artisans working at the looms, pottery wheels and goldsmithing. They had no idea how to reach the marketplaces of the world outside the village just waiting to pay affair price for the products they produced.

In the agriculture industry, I watched farmers cope with unpredictable access to water for irrigation, making it difficult to plan and produce good yields. For as long as I could remember, Mori had a system of gates that release water through canals to farmers, but farmers told me the water is not released when they need it, and sometimes no water is available. I would often hear talk about water, the main concern of farmers everywhere. In the back of my mind, he knew the number of suicides among these villagers, whose entire life was about farming, was increasing from their desperation and despair.

"The system for water distribution is not terrible" they would say to me. "It's too hard to figure out when the water will be turned on for the rice." There were no links between the point of control and the farmers. The timing for water distribution was too often done at the whim of the people controlling the flow, and it was difficult for farmers to plan. Distribution was another pain point. Getting coconuts to market was a constant problem. Supply chain issues at coconut farms compounded the low wages. Coconuts sell for 3 rupees (approximately 0.06) locally, but for 50 rupees (approximately 1.00) in the cities.

"We had a good number of coconuts this year. We did not get very much pay for them since the merchant taking them to the city wants to add so much to the price. It would be nice if we could sell direct but we don't know how."

Farmers lack access to current information on market prices for their crops and, as a result, often sell for less than they could. Thin margins mean farmers—80 percent of whom lease rather than own the land they farm—often struggle to make any profit after paying for supplies such as seeds and fertilizers. Also, the village's lack of cold storage facilities means a large share of what farmers do produce ultimately goes to waste

Some farmers I spoke with are trying to solve the problem by growing higher margin crops such as lentils, peanuts, sesame, and avocados. The environment is well suited to growing these. However, harvesting the higher value crops is very labor intensive, and emigration makes finding a sufficient number of workers difficult. People, especially young people, are leaving the village. Compounding the labor shortage are government programs. It is one of the unintended consequences of the government's attempt to help. Another example of short-term planning, a jobs program in Mori employs residents to dig canals, perform maintenance work, and other tasks. Although this program provides some value to the village, it is not a source of sustainable, demand-based employment growth. There is no real future. Because it is better than nothing, people take the jobs instead of going to work on the farms, where they would earn lower wages for more physically demanding work.

Crops are not the only thing farmed in Mori. Other villagers harvest shrimp, a high-margin product, from human-made ponds in the village. I would often wander by the ponds on my way to school where the shrimp farmers spent their days. They were large ponds tended by many villagers. I would watch them cast their nets to harvest the shrimp. The results were usually good, and the price of the shrimp was higher than anything else. There again the lack of good information put the ponds at risk from diseases that could have been prevented. Lack of access to information also prevented simple solutions that help limit the waste of precious water from the ponds as well.

Salt is added to the water in these ponds for the shrimp, which increases the salinity of the soil near the ponds and affects the rest of the village. Excess salts in soil hinder the growth of crops by limiting their ability take up water.

Digging the shrimp ponds, which must be deep to be effective, also draws seawater into the aquifer, further salinizing the soil and reducing yields for other crops, such as rice. Although shrimping near rice fields is banned to prevent salinization damage, according to what I learned from many villagers, it is still practiced. When there is little choice, people do what they need to survive.

I often heard of the conflicts between the shrimp farmers and the people growing rice. Even though shrimp farming was banned near rice paddies, the ponds were still placed in areas set aside for rice. Shrimp need salty water and rice need water that is clean and clear of salt. There was no plan, no strategy, no cooperation or communication, and that led to friction between the farmers.

Students were not the only one impacted adversely by the erratic bus schedules. Getting anywhere in the village, to a business or the clinic, as a project that often took an entire day. The lack of a set schedule for transportation made it almost impossible to travel to even see one of the few doctors, or go to the market, or into another part of the village to do business. Even when you manage to get to the bank, public office and or public utility, the lines are always long, and the wait plus travel time can take the better part of your day.

For most of my life, there were no telephones in the village. They recently started connected landlines, and the village was beginning to get mobile service the first time I returned as a professor from Berkeley. There was one internet center that was 3 miles from the center of the village. The population of 8,000 people had a total of 250 internet subscribers. In many ways, life in the village, like many villages in India and elsewhere, was cut off from the outside world.

These and other village conditions have caused many residents to leave, seeking better lives in some of India's large cities and the Middle East. They are likely to face substantial challenges in their new homes. Being a migrant created even greater challenges than leaving the village. If they had been able to stay many would have made that choice.

With opportunities lacking at home, the greatest irony is that many of the people with the most potential to improve village life are leaving. This trend exacerbates many problems, including the lack of teachers and local doctors.

For many people, all these pain points, these seemingly insurmountable challenges would have been overwhelming. Hearing them only strengthens my resolve that there was a solution. Based on what I heard, the issues seemed to fall into five broad groups:

1. Communication channels and open platforms within and outside the community.
2. Practical education and apprenticeships for self-development and to further their skills.
3. Tools and technology that empower will enable them to carry on their entrepreneurial activities.
4. Energy resources that are dependable and affordable to power their homes, shops, and schools.
5. Connectivity, affordable digital wireless connectivity that will save them costs and time and provide an invaluable connection to one another and the rest of the world.

It came down to these five important challenges. The villagers needed to be more effectively connected to each other and to the outside world, where there were markets for their goods, doctors for their health, and lessons for the students. The basic infrastructure of the village needed to be fixed and modernized with better more up-to-date systems for water, power, and sanitation. Current information and technology needed to be employed to help farmers farm more effectively to maximize their yields and sales from their harvests.

The technology which had been used and proven for many years, that was becoming so commonplace and widespread in urban areas, need to be brought to the village to increase connection, communication, collaboration, and cooperation. And this could not be a top-down effort. To succeed and be sustainable, the villagers needed to be the voice of the change, the brains behind the development and sustainable growth of the Smart Village. Every time I looked at all the problems, it the idea of the Smart Village became more real.

Chapter Five: The Smart Village Idea

On March 12, 2016, I was invited by the President of India to participate his Global Innovation Round Table at Rashtrapati Bhavan in New Delhi. It was here some of my ideas for Smart Villages were first expressed. It was the first time I talked about them to a group outside my small circle at Berkeley, and I want to share excerpts from my speech.

"I would like to thank the honorable President of India for inviting the Haas School of Business, University of California, Berkeley, to this most celebrated Global Innovation Round Table at Rashtrapati Bhavan. I would like to share with the distinguished guests around this table representing over 20 nations around the world, a few of my thoughts about the current education systems as it relates to emerging economies. My focus will be on the nature of delivery and access to the basic education available to the rural communities and its social-economic impacts on entrepreneurship and business opportunities, with a focus on India. I would like to draw your attention to the key problems based on our research and offer some possible solutions that some of us at Berkeley are trying to pivot and welcome your ideas and solutions.

I grew up in a small village in Andhra Pradesh, India. Back then my village was a clean and peaceful place with many hardworking people who labored in the field. I left my village as a teenager to the United States along with my dad who was offered a position as a scientist at the University of California. I returned to my village many times to find that there was little to no improvements. In many ways, things have gotten worse. The canals that I once swam and fished in are full of pollutants and plastic waste along with animal and human excretions. The roads are more crowded with autos and buses with a lot of noise and air pollution. Despite the number of schools that have come up, including the one I started, there is a high level of youth unemployment. I noticed that year after year farmers stopped growing their crops, as costs exceed revenues and suicide among them have gone up. Many who left the village to the Middle East to earn a better living through menial labor offer no incentive to family back home to work or improve their lives – many suffer from ailments of addictions and spend free living. I was told by my Chinese colleagues, the same is true in the villages in China with the migrant workers.

Close to 70% of the Indian population still live in villages. There are close to 650,000 villages in India and over 1 million villages in China.

Based on a survey done by my some of my students and validated by a previous survey done by the Andhra Pradesh government, the necessities like water and food, security, waste disposal, education and healthcare complicated by a high level of corruption are the major issues.

It is ironic that there have been many new advances in technology, new business model innovations and exponential growth in information and knowledge since I left my village as a teen. All this

48

progress did not offer many benefits to the rural populations where most of the people in the world live.

Our educational systems have failed us – they have not kept in synch with the changing landscape resulting from technology since the industrial era.

Education is all about the flow of knowledge – or access to knowledge as it is in the process of being created. Knowledge gives humans the power of invention and innovation to explore opportunities in creating value for them.

Knowledge is useless unless it flows in real time. Knowledge, I believe, must become a social good to benefit society across the silos and global barriers. When knowledge is held captive by the privileged class of a few – then inequity and injustice prevail.

Our solutions at UC Berkeley to the problems on the table comes from "Open Innovation." At UC Berkeley, we are firm believers in "Open Innovation" a concept that goes against base human nature to share, adapt and embrace change. UC Berkeley is the home of "Open Innovation" a word first coined by Professor Henry Chesbrough, whose research and work has been internationally recognized and applied.

Figure One: Open and Closed Innovation

Closed Innovation System
one way in and one way out
Knowledge is trapped in the funnel

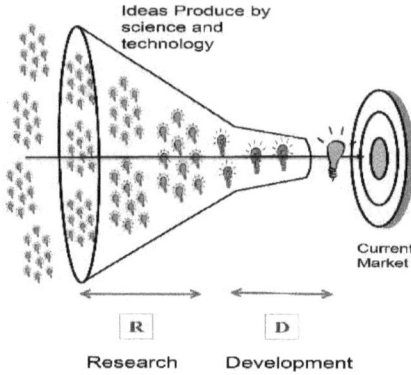

Ideas Produce by science and technology

Current Market

| R | D |

Research   Development

Open Innovation System
many ways in and many ways out
Knowledge flows in all directions improving speed to market

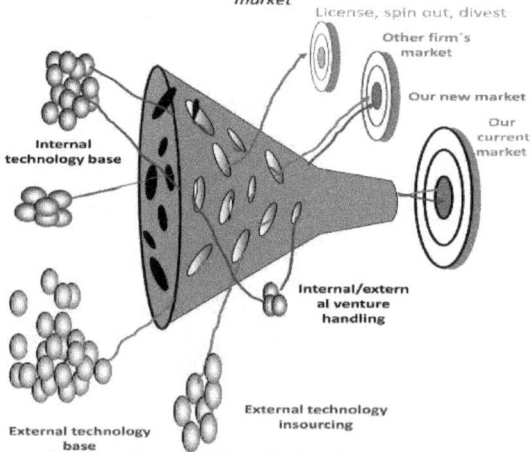

License, spin out, divest

Other firm's market

Our new market

Our current market

Internal technology base

Internal/external venture handling

External technology insourcing

External technology base

Stolen with pride from Prof Henry Chesbrough UC Berkeley, Open Innovation: Renewing Growth from Industrial R&D, 10th Annual Innovation Convergence, Minneapolis Sept 27, 2004

50

Professor Chesbrough initially conceived Open Innovation in Technology Development where entities and organizations benefited by sharing and exchanging knowledge. Today, Business Models, Services, and Marketing and the entire supply chain is applying this business model to capture full value. We are seeing its increasing significance in the development of public policy, the creation of Smart Cities and now Smart Villages.

Closed innovation seeks to hold knowledge captive and treat it as stock on the balance sheet while open innovation aims to facilitate the free flow of knowledge, breaking down silos, tightening the weakest links and relieving bottlenecks. Open Innovation is not merely soliciting and benefiting from other people's ideas - it is a two-way street. Both the giver and receiver have value to exchange. Knowledge flows both ways by creating a strategic advantage for both and establishes sustainable ecosystems. Increasingly, organizations that have embraced Open Innovation are experiencing significant improvement and flourishing in this current landscape.

Open Innovation is a solution to Indian Villages through a relevant educational system. We do not find most people in the villages wanting to earn graduate degrees and PhDs. It is not due to the lack of this kind of education. What they desire is enough practical education or information to help them. What I believe is needed in the basic educational system is for knowledge to be available for a rural population to empower and enable their natural abilities to improve their own lives and the lives of those around them.

A survey performed by our UC students among a cross-section of villagers who have a zeal to improve their living standards in their villages highlighted two key pain points.

1. *The lack of access to correct and timely information to create value for their businesses.*
2. *The lack of simple tools or basic training that will enable them to monetize the value they create for their customers.*

High levels of corruption and lack of transparency at all levels seemed to be bottlenecks and weakest links in the system and stop those who are willing to improve themselves. The farmer who is processing cashews in my village wants to know how he could package them and put them on the internet to make it available to the world. He is looking for simple, straightforward answers. He wants to know how he could register a business and get a license to export – whom to partner with and how to lower his cost to create value to the end consumer in the US.

A lady in my village who earns only $10 a saree she weaves on her vintage handloom machine wants to know how she could put her inventory on the internet – she is tired of earning the government set price of $10 for her saree that may take her a month to weave. Many of my friends in America feel $100 per saree is a steal for a beautifully crafted hand-woven cotton sari. She needs information and tools to do this.

It is this kind of education that is most needed in the 650,000 villages to bring about justice and equity in the system.

52

At UC Berkeley, I teach three relevant courses for our time:

1. *Business Models in Emerging Economies*
2. *Building Business Models Leveraging IBM Watson's Cognitive Analytics*
3. *Building Smart Cities.*

Last semester I challenged my students to utilize frugal but efficient technologies in making Visakhapatnam smart and wrapping a scalable and sustainable business model around them. The Chief Minister of Andhra Pradesh, India was impressed by my students work and presentations. He said to me privately "building a few Smart Cities is good but making a 1,000 villages smart will bring a much bigger bang to the GDP by economies of scale and scope."

I said that building Smart Villages are very doable in this age as there is no need for massive infrastructure, and digital tools are mostly free. The technology is already here that will promote transparency, speed of transaction, real-time communication, and most important of all cost elimination and time savings for the entire ecosystem.

Recently, I was appointed by him as the "Chief Innovation Officer" of the Andhra Pradesh government, which I accepted as an honorary position to help the country where I was born. Developing a prototype of a scalable and sustainable Smart Village in Mori is my first assignment. Developing a prototype Smart Village is the course I am offering this summer at Berkeley.

Developing this prototype is where I need all your help in the spirit of "Open Innovation." I would like to build a Smart Village as a platform that will capture the ideas from the global brain for implementation. Today's Education systems call for: Enablement, Empowerment, Exchange, Experimentation, and Encouragement for true learning to take place.

Helping me at UC Berkeley are many senior executives of global companies like Google, IBM, Ericsson, Cisco, Johnson Controls, GE, Qualcomm, Microsoft, SAP, Wipro, Hitachi, Dell-EMC, TechMahindra, Hella, and Usha in providing scaled down technologies at price points that villagers can afford. Scalability of these prototypes in these villages is what will drive future revenue growth for global multinational enterprises in the future."

This was the beginning, the start of the journey on the road to Mori, and the prototype for the Smart Village.

It is important to note at this point that the Mori Smart Village is not a place it is an idea. It is not a location, but a destination you want to reach. The first attempt to realize the idea was in Mori, India. That village represents villages everywhere, all 650,000 in India alone and over a million in countries around the world. Where did this idea originate? Many of us have heard about Smart Cities, but Smart Villages is a new idea. Why do we need Smart Villages?

The obvious answer is to make life better for the people living in these rural communities, improve how satisfied and happy they are. Yet, if that were the only reason, Smart Villages would not succeed. My experience in the disparate worlds of business and at academia led me to understand that companies needed new markets to continue growing, and the 3.4 billion people living in the villages of the world were an enormous untapped market opportunity.

A Smart Village would raise the happiness index, improve the standard of living and way of life, and do much more. It would need to be sustainable. To have a sustainable future, the community would also need to learn how to create *and* capture value, to be an economic development platform with a brand that identified their work. That meant the digital technologies needed to connect to the easily available knowledge and markets around the world. From my experience, I also understood that academia and government alone could not get the job done. I knew the effort required a business model, one that incorporated the expertise and experience business has developing, manufacturing, marketing, and selling products and services. The business model was the door to the enormous untapped markets the villages represented. My "Aha' moment came when I realized the model needed to be based on Open Innovation, an approach I learned from his friend Henry Chesbrough at the Haas School of Business. It was the final element that helped me see all the parts of Smart Village, an idea that was practical and sustainable whose time had come.

My working definition of a Smart Village became one that focuses on a community empowered by digital technologies and open innovation platforms with access to global markets. These Smart

Villages are a means of empowering people with access to tools, resources, real-time transparent information, using uninterrupted internet connectivity. My vision of what a Smart Village needed included six criteria that were critical for it to be successful. To decide whether or not a village has become a Smart Village, there must be an ecosystem, an economic development platform, a brand, a community, a business model, and a sustainable unit.

As an ecosystem, the Smart Village must leverage its resources, as well as those of surrounding villages, distant places, and other entities, to generate revenue and lower its costs and risk. Our human body is an ecosystem in which all individual organs work in perfect co-operation and coordination with each other creating, destroying, recycling and deploying substances when needed to sustain itself. This is done by producing and sharing resources that each other needs, using common distribution channels like the circulatory system for distribution, and the nervous system for communication.

There are many ideas that are being pivoted in the Smart Village of Mori. In villages, we are working with the taxi services to provide additional services as they drive around the village. When they are done picking up and dropping off passengers, we are also having them pick up groceries and supplies from local merchants and drop them off at doorsteps of people on their way for a small fee. Here all members of the ecosystem -- the taxi firm, the passenger, the merchant and customer who order the groceries or goods, the cell phone app company and the telecom service -- all benefit. Time is saved, costs are consolidated or eliminated, the risk is shared, the speed of service is improved, a higher number of transactions are generated, and for

56

some new revenues and services are created. All this is now enhanced with digital technology that offers platforms where the apps can reside on mobile devices offering the convenience of ordering on demand whenever wherever and however these services are needed.

To become an economic development platform, the Smart Village needs to allow external businesses access to its resources for both the businesses and the villagers to profit. This is the basis for the Co-Innovation approach to be viable. Village Digital Mall is a platform now being tested and developed by PayPal. Local rural merchants can put their products online to sell directly to households around the world for higher margins eliminating a host of intermediaries. Here everyone in the ecosystem benefits using this platform. All this happens by one click from a customer sitting on a couch in his living room in San Jose. For example, the customer shops on his computer and selects a product. That one click triggers a series of text messages to the village merchant in India, platform owner who fulfills the order, and to the transportation company. All this was impossible before seamless processes and networks were developed to orchestrate these activities.

As a brand, the Smart Village must learn to create an identity and become known for its unique value. For example, the weavers of Mori, who have perfected a unique art and producing for materials for thousands of years, need to brand their products and sell recognizable and need to sell recognizable and desirable vintage hand-loomed sarees "Made in Mori."

With connectivity and desperately needed access to information, the Smart Village is enabled and empowered to be a community that is a self-organized network of people who collaborate by sharing ideas, information, and resources to build a strong ecosystem. When projects fail, the community remains and rebuilds itself. The Smart Village community is more than any one project or program. The community is a group of people who adapt to changes in the marketplace and seek new ways of survival. A while back demand for rice export went down, but demand for shrimp farming went up. The community was able to adapt and switch their investments and form new ecosystems to meet this demand. Now with the availability of digital technologies, this can happen more efficiently empowering the whole ecosystem.

To become a business model, the Smart Village must create value for its people and others outside the village by utilizing lean and cost-effective state-of-the-art technologies. The Village business model is composed of the sum of its business activities taking place within itself. This means the village should offer an efficient digital infrastructure to its business to generate profits and cut costs by promoting and supporting platforms and formation of ecosystems. For example, the first thing we did in Mori is to provide internet and cell phones to every household to provide global access to everyone to begin to communicate, setup a business, and make transactions. This is the first step in laying the foundation to build business models. An individual business in a village will need to address the pain points of its customers to create value.

To create value, it needs to leverage its ecosystem around it to be profitable. It needs to secure resources, generate activities and form partnerships, in a cost-effective manner, to address the needs of its customers. The village, with its many businesses operating within it, should capture some of the value it creates for itself in terms of profit or taxes. Thinking in terms of a business model makes villages more sustainable and self-contained. This reduces its dependence on the State and the Central Governments and reduces emigration of its human capital to cities. In a sense, Sir Arthur Cotton did create what was at that point in history, "Smart Villages" with technology available to his generation, but the world and the technology has greatly changed since then. In this era, we need to adapt our village business models by incorporating digital technologies to create value.

Finally, the Smart Village grows to be a sustainable unit. That means that the village operates using a multiple-bottom-line approach, focusing on people, profit, the planet, partnership, and prosperity. All aspects of the bottom-line need to be part of the equation and equally considered for a balanced and sustainable future to happen. This means that we need to develop models that will not destroy our planet. Profitability and scalability of businesses should not be the enemy of sustainability.

The school kids in Mori at the Smart Village exhibition proposed that their village roads should not allow patrol or diesel vehicles to travel within the village. They also proposed to ban the local cashew processing factories that produce excessive carbon emissions. A sustainable unit is governed by good policies and technologies that improve the happiness and health of local people, generates economic profit, promotes a green planet, provides equitable profit sharing to its ecosystem partners and builds a prosperous community where people do not seek to emigrate elsewhere. All this is possible with today's technology.

This would be a dramatic change for the villagers, to let go of the way they worked and lived for their whole lives. I also knew from talking with them that they were more than ready for the journey. To help them understand what would be involved, I explained there were many important connections between where they were, and where they wanted to go. The answers were not to simply add technology or information. There was a logic in my mind that defined the road to a Smart Village. That logic became the guidelines I shared about what it takes to create a Smart Village. The regression from data to happiness became a simple set of steps to follow.

Data is *useless* unless it is converted into Information. We live in a world in which data has become the basic currency. In the past, it might have land or things, but now it is data. And data is just that, a lot of little bits, ones and zeroes in a digital world, and it leads to facts and then becomes information. Data alone is useless it becomes information.

Information is *useless* unless it is converted into knowledge. Once data is transformed into information, it needs another step to make it useful. Information needs to be found, curated, read, understood and transferred as knowledge to make it useful to people. Information to help the weavers find markets, the rice farmers to preserve precious water, the shrimp farmers to avoid disease. Information was a key, but

60

information alone is useless. Information needs to be turned into knowledge.

Knowledge is *useless* unless it produces something useful, and that means in a Smart Village, a useful way of doing things. This can be a new approach or a new technology that helps to improve the way work is done or how peoplele live. Knowledge is useless unless it flows in society. The old idea that "knowledge is power" and that it needs to be hoarded is destructive and disabling to a smart society. The new idea that "shared knowledge is the real power" needs to take hold. A Smart Village is an open society in which knowledge flows freely from one person to another, connecting their minds, enriching their lives, providing the basis for sharing, collaborating and communicating. Knowledge needs to be transformed into technology.

To take it step further, technology is *useless* without a business model. Unless there is a business model that involves the potential users in a way to help that technology be valuable and useful, places a monetary value on the technology, and locates a market in which it can be found and sold, the technology is useless. Without a business model to make the technology into a useful product or service, the only purpose it will have will be as a display in a technology museum.

Even the business model is *useless* unless it is sustainable and scalable. Once the technology has a business model, the next step is for that model to be sustainable. Sustainable means that the model needs to be able to go forward in time and be as useful tomorrow as it is today. That means it can be repaired if needed and easily replaced when needed. Scalability is useless if it becomes the enemy of sustainability. The downside to scalability is that the business model and the technology it offers can be scaled too much, it can grow too fast. When that happens, it becomes a problem for sustainability because there are issues with quality and reparability, and the shelf life and usefulness of the technology is limited. Plus, scalability can get in the way of the long-term goal of continuous improvement if the short-term goal is to keep making as many things as possible. Both sustainability and scalability need to work together for the business model to be dynamic and successful.

Ultimately, the point is to improve the happiness index of people. Data can be transformed into knowledge, and the resulting technology can be made useful by a scalable and sustainable business model, yet none of is worth very much unless it adds to the happiness of the people. In the final analysis, it is the happiness of the people that must override everything else. And that happiness is tied up in the ability of the community to be part of the process that takes them from all the data to happiness.

Chapter Six: Smart Village Business Models and Open Innovation

My grandmother living in a segregated society in Mori experienced the power of Open Innovation under the most disastrous circumstances. While she was attempting to end her life due to lack of hope, an Englishman missionary named Charles Whitehouse saved her life from drowning. As she and her caste were denied educational rights, Charles gave her refuge and taught her and her husband basic math and how to read and write. In Open Innovation terms, this is knowledge acquired in the UK flowing into the minds of simple villagers in India. Given the constraints of conducting business or trade in the village due to their caste, they established trade outside the country. A few lessons from Charles helped my grandfather get a job as Payroll Manager in Burma and helped my grandmother develop several businesses outside the country to beat the caste system.

In Open Innovation terms, knowledge flowed IN from England and knowledge flowed OUT from my grandmother through training many untouchable women to learn the new trade of exported lace products back to England. She also taught weavers to export handloom textiles from the village to Burma. She became the largest employer in the village and disrupted the local landlords' business models. Women switched over from doing scavenger work to doing lace and exports that is far more lucrative and dignifying than their horrible birthright

Just like Charles Whitehouse learned the local language and got to know people in the village to help them and enable them, corporations will need to do the same today to unlock growth opportunities in emerging markets. Open Innovation works even under the worst of circumstances if there are small openings for knowledge to flow outside IN and inside OUT. With digital gateways today, the possibilities to empower people are endless.

Open Innovation demands execution capabilities, and this requires wise and adaptable leadership. I had always been fascinated by the name that my father gave me "Solomon Darwin" which consists of two significant people in history who are diabolically opposite of one another in their backgrounds. I have found that my name carried two ingredients to succeed in life.

"Where there is no vision people perish." *King Solomon*

"It is not the strongest of the species that survives, nor the most intelligent that survives. It is the one that is most adaptable to change." *Charles Darwin*

Solomon the Wise was the most successful king in Israel's history. His leadership approach brought his nation to its zenith of economic prosperity. Unlike his father King David, he never fought a single war in his life. Instead, he brought the enemies of this father to the peace table and collaborated with them. He developed business ecosystems to create prosperity for all through banking, trade, and commerce. Our Jewish settlements in India go back to the time of King Solomon where he traded with the Maharajas of India. He traded horses in exchange for silk, spices, precious stones and the services of great architects. He was truly an Open Innovation King. The success of his leadership style is casting a clear vision that galvanized his people and the nations of the world around him, to work with him. This required Open Innovation thinking.

Darwin, writing about the survival of the fittest, stated that unless we adapt and respond to the changing landscape, we perish. This also requires Open Innovation thinking.

*Both concepts, **Vision** which means seeing the direction in which we want to move, and **Adaptability** which means being able to respond to changes quickly, require corporate leadership capabilities and strategies beyond the ordinary – they are both "Dynamic Capabilities."*

In my experience dealing with governments, the Open Innovation and corporate leadership capabilities and strategies I describe do not work well unless there are collaborative structure and process that brings the government entities (catalysts), universities (knowledge creators) and business enterprises (job creators) together. This is what I call the "Triple Helix Model."

These three elements - Open Innovation, Dynamic Capabilities, and Triple Helix - are essential ingredients that make business models successful, expand rural economies, and create Smart Villages.

Figure Two: Dynamic Capabilities

A Paradigm Shift
From Resources to Dynamic
Capabilities

OLD WAY

NEW WAY

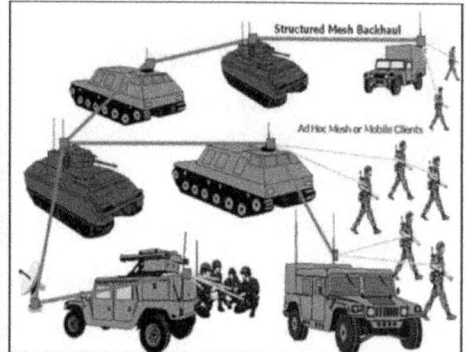

Balance sheet" view of
assets and capabilities

Little emphasis on
"orchestration" as the key
success factor.

Heavy emphasis on soft assets
which assist in orchestrating
deployment and
redeployment

Key Success Factor: Rapid
deployment

What is essential is no longer on the balance sheet –
capabilities of an organization have migrated to
people enabled by the digital technology.

Source: David Teece

Minister Naidu, Chief Minister of Andhra Pradesh, embraced these three concepts and paved the way for the Smart Village Movement in India. On a warm day late in December 2016, Chief Minister Naidu came to Mori where more than 40,000 villagers were waiting. That day, 80 executives, many representing global brands, presented the technologies they developed for the prototype Smart Village.

He was most impressed with over 40 companies successfully coming together and collaborating in this remote village. After hearing the presentations, he invited the executives who were available and me to see him the following day at his office over three hours away in Vijayawada.

I gave two-hour lecture presentation about the four frameworks I employed - Open Innovation, Dynamic Capabilities, Triple Helix and Business Model – that was making the prototype Smart Village in Mori a success -. At the end of the presentation, he made a request. He asked me to expand the work to 476 villages in five critical districts in his state of Andhra Pradesh as well.

Later that day, his aids told me that it was the first and perhaps only time they watched him sit through a two-hour lecture, listening carefully, and taking notes.

On September 7, 2016 Mori, during the beginning of our smart village project, *the government gave me the pleasure of turning on the switch the provided internet connection to every home in Mori. This one single act of flipping the switch generated feeling that I cannot describe in words – this is the remote place where I grew up that was devoid of so many privileges during my lifetime and generations before me. This was an inspirational moment and was so liberating.*

We heard story after story from people - within the first-hour people started streaming You-Tube video live, students doing homework, merchant transactions and cash transfers were facilitated. This connectivity helped my team to perform healthcare and agriculture pilots, and later in December, they began the drive to make Mori the first cashless village.

Here is the best story yet. When I turned on that switch on September 7, 2016, the first person to get on Skype was a disabled kid who was deaf and dumb, who communicated unspeakable joy in sign language upon seeing his best friend in Canada on his computer screen. This access to the flow of two-way communication facilitates not just innovation but also the inspiration for people who need hope. Like this kid who had been depressed and lonely most of this life, he found new ways to express himself to his long-lost friend on the other side of the world. With digital gateways today, the possibilities to empower people are endless.

It was critical to complete a working definition of a Smart Village at this point before we began to develop the prototype in Mori. Early on, the definition focused on empowering the community using always-on digital technologies. That was too close what many call bridging "the digital divide." That alone was not enough not make a village and villagers "smart." Smart Villages are not about providing simple point solutions such as access to the internet and internet-capable devices.

It is important to understand Open Innovation and its role in building smart villages. Professor Henry Chesbrough[7], faculty director of the Haas Center for Open Innovation, is the "Father of Open Innovation." When I met him, according to Henry, "It was a fortuitous meeting, for it catalyzed the transformation of Professor Darwin's thinking, and provided a powerful concept to unlock a new approach to rural development." And it was true.

Henry defined the term in his book *Open Innovation: The new imperative for creating and profiting from technology*[8]. Open innovation was first defined in the book as "a paradigm that assumes that firms can and should use external ideas as well as internal ideas, and internal and external paths to market, as the firms look to advance their technology."[9]

The issue for Smart Villages is that companies typically take a closed approach to innovation. Companies employ a research and development team--often several in different parts of the company—who generate and refine ideas into products and services for end markets, whether they are consumers or other businesses. In open innovation, companies both take in external ideas and make their ideas available for others to build upon. This flow of ideas is a win-win that benefits the company by including the input of the consumer's real needs and is of great benefit to the consumer since the products and services that are produced more effectively meet their real needs. This is especially true in today's environment in which information flows freely and in every direction. Since innovation faster than ever before, with ideas and inventions coming from everywhere all the time, the shelf life of a company's intellectual property (IP) has greatly decreased. Instead of locking that IP away forever, it makes more sense to share it with the world and find someone who uncovers a new use and market for it.

This old model developed during the Industrial Revolution when business models and the output of R&D were closed off from one another. Innovation was considered a secret and highly competitive edge. Even within a company siloes of R&D information in different groups or divisions were guarded and closely held. The basic operating principle held that knowledge was power. In this relatively new knowledge economy, the basic belief idea for operating a company is that sharing knowledge is power. This leads to a more open way of doing business in which innovation happens from all sides – inside the company as well as outside with customers and even competitors.

For example, a company may license technology from another company and develop it into a new product. Or the company may enter into a joint venture or other agreement with an external firm to co-develop the idea into a product or service. Firms leveraging open innovation may also make their unused patents or ideas available to outside companies or other entities interested in developing products or services.

Another facet of a closed business model is that businesses tend to employ and depend on current technologies. To succeed in this knowledge economy, businesses need to start exploring and depending on the future, on technologies that are anticipated to become important for products and services. Again, the only way to successfully do this is through open innovation in which the collective and collaborative intelligence is captured. In the environment today, which is more transparent and collaborative, open innovation recognizes that it is more efficient to incorporate people outside the company – in this case, the villagers of Mori – to discover what they need and use their knowledge and experience to co-create new products and services.

According to Henry Chesbrough, "Open innovation is based on the concept of harnessing knowledge flowing from the outside in one's innovation processes and allowing unused knowledge to flow outside for others to use in their innovations. In other words, one doesn't have to do everything on one's own. One can harness the knowledge and skills of others in the process of innovation."

Building Smart Villages are very doable in this age as there is no need for heavy infrastructure, and digital tools are essentially free. The technology is already here that will promote transparency, the speed of transaction, real-time communication, effective pivots, and most important of all cost elimination and time savings for the entire Smart Village and the companies that have the vision to service them. Transitioning to a Smart Village smart is intended to enable villagers to become economically independent while simultaneously creating business opportunities for firms bringing products and services to the village.

At a very basic level, the competitiveness of a company and the health of the communities around it are closely intertwined. A business needs a successful community, not only to create demand for its products but also to provide critical public assets and a supportive environment. A community needs successful businesses to provide jobs and wealth creation opportunities for its citizens.

The focus of Smart Villages is to design a business process for external resource providers like technology firms to innovate and develop the products and services with villagers. The goal is straightforward. Help the providers build viable products and services that address the pain points of the villagers' everyday life. Sustain the village over time as an ecosystem, a community, a brand, and a platform as well as a business model. In the Smart Village prototype, Open Innovation evolved into a very specific application – Co-Innovation.

As of now, over 22 firms are involved in prototyping, including many prominent Silicon Valley firms. The model that was proposed offers multinational firms the opportunity to generate profits for themselves as they scale their business models derived from their co-innovation efforts to the rest of the 38,000 villages. The nation will benefit as the firms extend their models beyond the state to the rest of India's 650,000 villages. That represents a huge market for new co-innovated products and services. Both the firms and villagers will benefit from this bottom-up approach, which will leverage both the economies of scale and scope resulting in improving the level of happiness of the village population.

The Smart Village business model took Open Innovation and Co-Innovation one step further and created Co-Innovation Labs where the people of Mori and the 22 global corporations participating in the program could meet, discuss the pain points, and come up with ideas that ultimately become products and services.

As one among many examples, after working with people in the Co-Innovation Lab, PayPal developed the Digital Mall for Mori that residents. With a simple mobile phone and an entrepreneurial spirit, anyone could create a bank account, get paid for work they did or things they made, and make deposits. Those deposits then became transferable for other needed goods and services. Where there once was no easy way to use a bank, a simple digital and mobile solution began to create a thriving economy. The next step is to answer several questions. Is the Digital Mall scalable? How far beyond Mori can the solution reach? Is Mori representative of villages everywhere? Will this new business model work in other parts of India or other rural villages throughout the world?

The Smart village is one of the greatest opportunities for global brands to expand into the emerging market of villages around the world. To be successful entering these new markets, companies must pursue business models that include a combination of this untraditional business framework as well as these new approaches including Open Innovation, Co-Innovation, low price-high value products, and a Fair Value Model.

Execution of Open Innovation requires the right leadership, and the creation of Smart Villages requires a new mindset. That mindset requires more than the ability to organize and manage. It requires a paradigm shift in thinking and approach. Smart Village leadership requires the ability to have a vision and to galvanize everyone to make that vision a reality. Rapidly adapting to changes as they happen is not easy, yet it is the key to success. These new leadership capabilities, incorporating these Open Innovation approaches, is a dramatic change from traditional approaches and is critical requirement needed to expand markets in this digital age.

Professor David Teece, from the Haas School of Business, makes a good comparison of this paradigm shift. In the past, the balance sheet view emphasized a focus on assets owned to develop a product. That was the way the product development was traditionally viewed. The new way is to get access to assets rather than ownership of assets. Uberization is not new in villages. When I was growing up, my village had only one of everything. One family owned a stone grinder, and another owned a flour strainer. We circulated them around instead of each family buying their own. In rural villages, assets "sweat" from being in almost constant demand. This eliminates the need for investment costs and lowers the risk.

This approach is important as we move into the digital knowledge economy, because the value of technology or intellectual assets evaporate very quickly, unlike physical assets which we can touch and feel. Ownership is less valuable than access. Today is all about access to more soft and mobile assets that a company may not even own. And this makes the differences between old and new approaches very apparent.

The traditional way of doing business requires the ability to manage a large organization and effectively operate a hierarchical chain of command. The old way of leadership required more traditional capabilities including operating, administrating, and

74

governing. This type of leadership is all about **"doing things right"** which is easily imitated and managed. The new approach, suited for a Smart Village prototype, requires different capabilities in leadership. It is all about quickly adapting and orchestrating a rapid deployment and redeployment in response to the changing environment. The new way calls for much more dynamic capabilities - adapting, integrating, sensing, ceasing and transforming. In short, being able to successfully and continuously pivot. The new approach is all about **"doing the right thing."** This is a big difference in leadership styles and one that was highlighted as the Smart Village evolved.

For open innovation and co-innovation processes to be successful, there needs to be a model within which businesses, schools, and governments operate as equals, to deliver maximum efficiency and effectiveness to society. That model is the Triple Helix powered by Open Innovation and Co-Innovation, in which knowledge transfer is maximized and supported by all three stakeholders. The Triple Helix Model of Open Innovation refers to the interactions between academia, industry, and governments that foster economic and social development. This framework was first theorized by Henry Etzkowitz[10] and Loet Leydesdorff[11] in the 1990s.

Closed innovation worked in the past before the internet, when there was no way for companies, customers and even competitors to communicate. In a sense, there was no plumbing for knowledge to flow through the pipes. The model of the Triple Helix only works with Open Innovation, where knowledge needs flow in real time to achieve speed to market for a competitive advantage.

Figure Three: Triple Helix Model

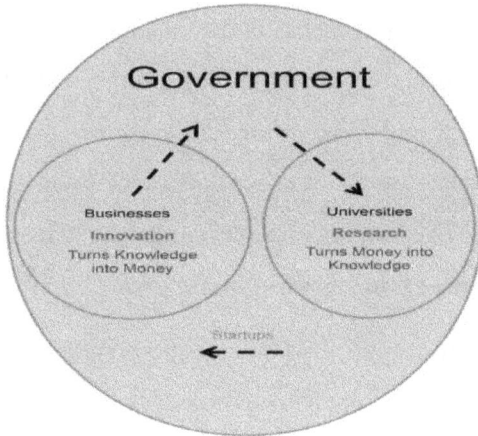

When Triple Helix Does Not Work
Circles are not equal

Government

Businesses
Innovation
Turns Knowledge into Money

Universities
Research
Turns Money into Knowledge

Startups

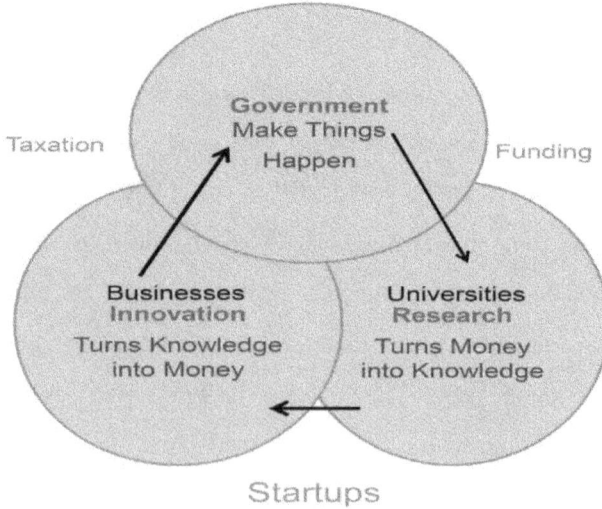

Triple Helix Framework
Knowledge Generation, Deployment & Capture

Taxation

Government
Make Things Happen

Funding

Businesses
Innovation
Turns Knowledge into Money

Universities
Research
Turns Money into Knowledge

Startups

Because of globalization and the spread of digital technology, innovation is happening faster than ever and can originate from any point on the planet. Companies can no longer depend on their current products and services based on today's technology. They must begin to innovate and co-innovate to develop the technologies of tomorrow. Innovation cannot happen in a vacuum. Businesses need the help of government and academia. These three key stakeholders need to be equal partners. They need to leverage the Triple Helix Model in which open communication and collaboration occurs between government, academia, and business. Each has a role to play.

Government is a key player and needs to be the catalyst and provide incentives for innovation and co-innovation as well as remove any regulations that get in the way and disable the innovation process. The government needs to provide incentives for innovation in the form of funding and grants for research, and special tax incentives at the local and regional levels. Their policy towards the schools needs to be one that facilitates and open exchange of information. This means that even if funding comes from the government in the form of public education, they need to have the same hands-off policy that privately funded colleges and universities have about research projects.

The key to the level of research that occurs in academia is directly related to the level of freedom from government interference they must pursue the research they – or their business partners – deem worth pursuing. The laws governing the patents and use of research that was done with government funds by a university or college need to be viewed through the modern lens of open innovation.

The role of government in the development of Silicon Valley companies is an example. Knowledge of many of the basic technology was created when government invested funding to these universities. As an example of the results, 70% of the early Ph.D. theses in the sciences were classified as top secret. Downstream from the innovation, the government provided investment and tax incentives to commercialize the knowledge and create jobs. Jobs that generated taxpayers by which the government gets paid back. The caveat is that for this work, all parts of the circle need to be relatively equal which most countries are unable to achieve because of their cultural, political or ideological mindset.

Academia must support an open exchange of ideas and be the risk-taker in experimenting and researching areas that might not have any immediate or obvious return-on-investment of time and money. The labs in the universities and colleges need to focus on ideas and projects and provide the education, and resources needed for basic research. Senior managers and executives also need to be educated by schools about ways to be more open and innovative, and the movement of personnel between businesses and schools is an important part of the transfer of knowledge.

There is also the opportunity for co-op programs between the schools and the businesses where they can work and learn together. In the Knowledge Economy, in which innovation is increasingly a function of the knowledge created through research done by universities and colleges, academia plays a more co-equal role than ever before.

Business does what it does best and monetizes and commercializes the ideas that come out of the research academia produces and are helped to market by government rules and regulations. Business can provide funding for projects in academia as well as establish strong and lasting relationships with a university or college. Businesses can also enter into a partnership with a university or college and create an ongoing research program.

The Triple Helix Model gives Open Innovation leverage to solve the world's most pressing challenges, including global health, water, energy, environment, food, education, security, and poverty. The Open Innovation process provides cost-effective and sustainable solutions, capturing the work and support of government, academia, and business.

The Triple Helix Model assumes that research and the resulting innovations are part of a developed economy in which economic growth is a function of a market-based economy where the innovations can find consumers. It also presupposes that the role of government is to protect the resulting innovations by providing laws for the intellectual property. Until recently, the triple helix model, overlapping the government, academia and business only worked in countries where all three stakeholders were able to operate freely and would not be viable in a developing country like India. What was missing was co-innovation where the people are a fourth dimension in the helix structure.

The success of the Triple Helix Model was first apparent in healthcare for the Smart Village of Mori and the telemedicine projects led by the Smart Village Team and Dr. Swati Subodh. It began with free screenings in Mori's co-innovation lab that were part of the prototyping of the healthcare initiative. To spread the idea out across the village, eight Aanganwadi ("shelter) teachers hosted telemedicine clinics in their centers. It was another example of the way that women are being empowered in the village to make Mori smart.

The Cloud Physician and Health Care ATM with a healthcare provider is another example of the Triple Helix Model at work. Healthcare in India is a national crisis. The doctor-patient ratio is a shocking 1:1,700. To make matters worse, 80% of Indian doctors are located in urban areas serving only 28% of the populace.

According to Venkata Krishna Kagga, a Smart Village Fellow from the University of California, "As we started interacting with villagers and local politicians, we noticed the seriousness of the bad situation in the Indian health sector. The idea of this healthcare model started with the question, is it possible for the 20% of the doctors[12] to address the needs of 72% of the Indian population that lives in a rural setting?

We came to an understanding that this can only be achieved by strengthening the existing system by equipping the rural healthcare workers with advanced technologies and imparting knowledge and skills needed to leverage on technological advancements from the healthcare Industry. Our journey began, and it showed me what innovative ways along with technology could achieve to benefit society."

After the Smart Village Team from UC Berkeley worked with the community to identify their pain points - Access, Affordability, Accountability and Quality -- an innovative approach was developed to offer healthcare services at villager's doorstep through cloud-based physicians and by leveraging the existing system of healthcare workers.

Several healthcare technology companies from Silicon Valley and Indian healthcare providers were explored. Yolo healthcare ATM are currently being deployed for pivoting to develop a viable business model. The villagers, the Mori Smart Village team, representatives from the government and all the partnering companies are all working together in concert as equal partners on the way the program meets the needs and solves the pain points of the villagers now and into the future.

A detailed case study (see Appendix 3) was developed for the Roadmap covering the entire process of Open Innovation and the development of the Cloud Physician project.

Because villagers typically have very low incomes, the products and services that can both improve their lives and fit within their budgets must come at a low price and provide high value. To meet both those criteria, companies must innovate rather than rely on a basic strategy of either product differentiation or cost leadership. They must take an uncommon approach to innovating. Rather than adding new features, they must remain focused on simplicity.

For example, an electrocardiograph (ECG), a machine used to record heart activity, costs thousands of dollars and requires reliable electricity. A full-sized machine would need to be transported by truck to its destination, and it would need to be operated by a skilled technician. A highly educated cardiologist or another medical professional then interprets the results.

Many villages lack not just the funds to purchase such equipment for the local hospital, but also everything else necessary for the machine to serve its purpose, including easily passable roads in and out for the delivery truck. To address this need, General Electric created the MAC 400, a simplified, low-cost ECG that runs on batteries and is small enough and light enough to be portable. Since introducing the MAC 400 in 2007, GE has expanded its line of low-cost ECGs by refining the design to meet the needs of villagers and villages more effectively. By 2011, total sales in the MAC line exceeded 10,000 units.

Porter and Kramer have developed what they call the Fair Value Model which extends the idea of simple co-innovation even further. They conclude that reimagining the value chains, from the perspective of a Smart Village, to provide the maximum in shared value, will offer significant new ways to innovate and unlock new economic value that most businesses have missed.

For companies, the first step in pursuing a Fair Value Model and providing shared value opportunities is assessing their products and services in terms of how they address or create societal needs, benefits, and harms.

As an example, Thomson Reuters has developed a promising monthly service for farmers who earn an average of $2,000 a year. For a fee of $5 a quarter, it provides weather and crop-pricing information and agricultural advice. The service reaches an estimated two million farmers, and early research indicates that it has helped increase the incomes of more than 60 percent of them—in some cases tripling incomes.

Through a combination of all these business models and approaches including innovation, co-innovation, low price-high value product pricing, and a Fair Value Model, the final piece of the Smart Village model is brought to bear making the prototype scalable and sustainable. The approaches help further define the sustainability and growth of a Smart Village: A community using digital technologies in concert with open innovation platforms that can access global markets.

To make the Smart Village attractive to corporations, they must be scalable. What are the primary obstacles to scaling, and how can they be overcome? Currently, the program approach is slightly fragmented, as there is a different partner for each village. The biggest challenge for the program is to create a single communications platform that models in real time the challenges and showcases the success stories, motivating partners in villages across the state to copy the success in the villages in which they are working.

The key objective of the program is to bring in a shared, holistic approach, with a spirit of common good. At the same time, it is imperative to avoid the following:

- Top-down approach from a single source either government or corporate that ends up driving the project
- Leakage of funds through a lack of oversight or good accounting
- Lack of effective communication between the various stakeholders including villages, village leaders, government leaders and corporations
- Avoiding political interference in the implementation process through unnecessary regulations or guidelines imposed by the state.

It cannot be business as usual and must take an out-of-the-box imaginative approach to succeed.

Every business in a Smart Village needs to address the pain points of their customers to create value. To create value, it needs to leverage the customers, employees, and even competitors to be profitable. It needs to secure resources, generate activities, and form partnerships to meet the needs of its customers cost-effectively. As a business model, the Smart Village, with its many businesses, needs to capture some of the value it creates as economic profit. Thinking in terms of a business model makes Smart Villages more sustainable and self-contained.

After more than three years or thinking, discussing and refining – plus a most auspicious meeting with Professor Henry Chesbrough – the definition that would drive our work and turn Mori into the first Smart Village began to feel solid. To be a Smart Village, the entire community requires more than access to always-on digital technology. I realized that the access needs to be combined with open innovation platforms that can facilitate open innovation processes and allow many ecosystem players, from customers to employees, and even competitors to build upon it. Because only by being open and generating traction for stakeholders can these Smart Villages create an ongoing, evolving community of users who continuously adapt and change to maintain their value.

Open innovation platforms do not attempt to provide an end-to-end solution, but facilities open innovation with as few barriers as possible. These platforms are critical for another reason as well. They generate a network effect through onboarding as people sign-on as users. As the platforms get used, more people use it, and the interest compounds.

Open Innovation became a critical piece of the definition and formed the basis for the business model. The Smart Village must create value for people in the village as well as outside by utilizing lean, cost-effective state-of-the-art technologies to be a business model. The village must offer an efficient digital infrastructure to its businesses for them to operate effectively, getting and keeping customers, listening to their customers, improving the customer experience, generating profits and cutting costs. The first step taken toward building workable business models in Mori was to provide internet connectivity and cell phones for every household. This enables everyone to communicate, collaborate, establish businesses, and make transactions. The business framework was the next piece to put into place.

In my conversations with Henry, we talked a great deal about the need for new approaches to make the Smart Village idea a reality.

Henry summed it up when we compared old and new models of doing business.

According to Henry, "Earlier approaches to rural development were predicated on the idea of market failure. There wasn't enough income in rural areas to attract companies and markets to engage with them, beyond the rudiments of subsistence agriculture. A new approach is needed, to break the cycle of rural poverty, empower individuals to grow their skills, access markets, overcome corruption, and scale beyond the initial area where assistance was received."

Generating wealth from people at the bottom pyramid cannot be achieved without open innovation and open business models. The reason is simple: The current business models, that are based on a closed system of innovation, in which discoveries and the resulting products and services are developed "in-house" will not work. It is impossible for a company in a developed world to understand the needs of the people who live and work in villages in the developing world. The need to open the process of innovation and the model for doing business to include the people is necessary if both the businesses and the people are to prosper.

The village is a business model that creates value to for those outside its ecosystem (borders) as well as capture some of the value to sustain its internal ecosystem of many businesses operating within it. Local governments and landlords run villages, and there is no room for innovative ideas to create new products and services to take root and blossom. Many ideas and efforts die on the vine, and there is no

86

structure in place to capture new ideas, knowledge, and information. This insight was crucial to the success of the Smart Villages.

The old traditional business model focuses on pushing products and services to the customers. This Push Business Model (Figure Four) does not create enough value for the customers and would not work in the Smart Villages in India or around the world. It is all about the corporation identifying the needs of a customer—often assuming that they know the pain points and solution--and investing in resources and activities, and finding partners then trying to push the value to the customer like the door-to-door salesperson. We needed a model that would listen to and understand and solve the pain points and support the innovativeness of the village community.

On the other hand, the Pull Business Model (Figure Five) is based on the approaches used with Open Innovation to create value. In this model, there is little investment in purchasing balance sheet assets that reside (or are fixed) at a single location. The investment is on utilizing global assets, mobile cloud-based resources, activities, and partners from a wide variety of open innovation platforms and networks. The results are products and services truly based on customers real needs and demands.

The Pull Business Model cuts down on developmental costs since there is no need to reinvent the wheel or build it – we borrow the one that already exists. Here, a customer only pays for what they use based on their changing real-time needs and not for someone else's dead assets or shelf space.

Figure Four: Push Business Model

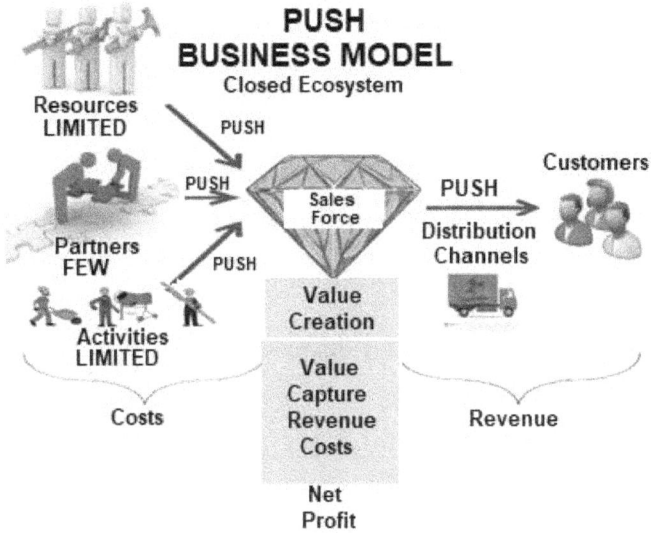

PUSH BUSINESS MODEL
Closed Ecosystem

Resources LIMITED — PUSH
PUSH — Sales Force
Partners FEW — PUSH
PUSH — Distribution Channels
Activities LIMITED
Value Creation
Value Capture Revenue Costs
Costs
Revenue
Customers
Net Profit

Figure Five: Pull Business Model

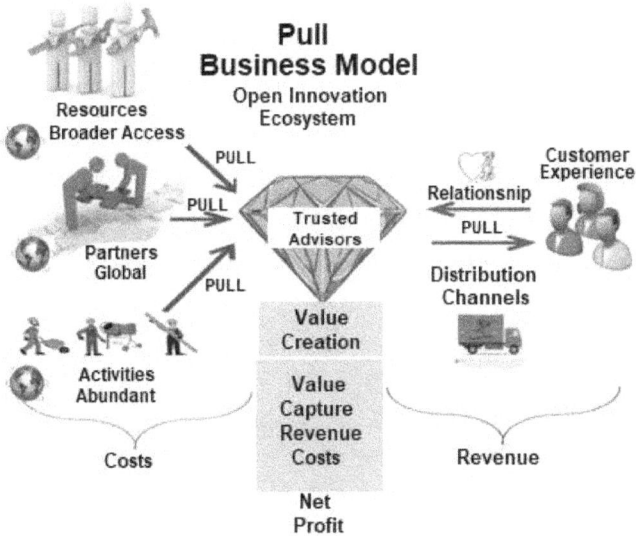

Pull Business Model
Open Innovation Ecosystem

Resources Broader Access — PULL
PULL — Trusted Advisors
Partners Global — PULL
Relationsnip — PULL
Distribution Channels
Activities Abundant
Value Creation
Value Capture Revenue Costs
Costs
Revenue
Customer Experience
Net Profit

.It's a utility-based pricing model that is more agile and adaptable, delivering a higher quality product. A product that saves time on both sides (consumer and producer) eliminate costs, reduces risk, lowers costs as the platform gains traction, attracts and retains talent for the business, and increased customer retention and happiness. It is a model ideally suited for corporations to develop products and services for a Smart Village.

An integral part of the Pull Business Model is that it is based on pivoting to co-create products and services with the customer. Instead of pushing products to customers, the customers pull us to meet their demands (Figure Six).

Figure Six: The Pivot Process

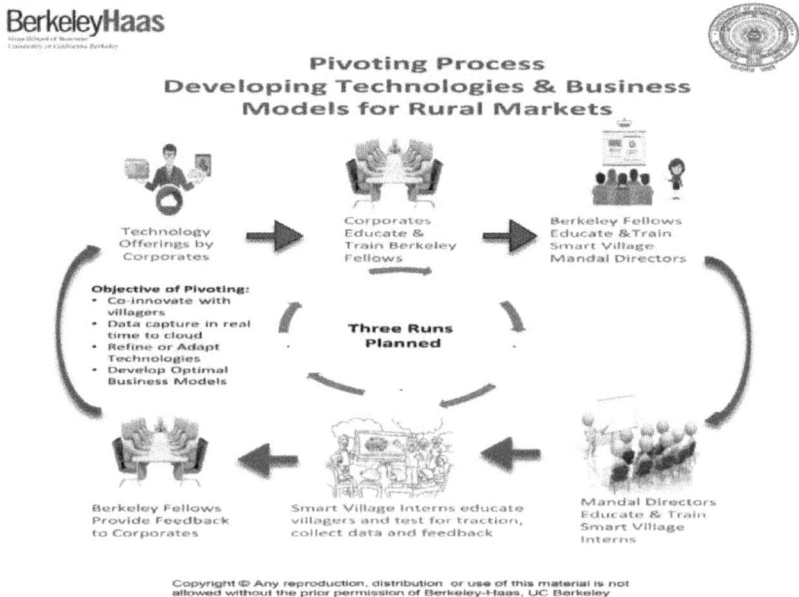

Pivoting is an action taken when you discover that your hypotheses do not meet reality. Open Innovation and the Pull model between villagers and companies require many iterations to fine-tune a technology and result in a sustainable and scalable business model. The objective is to generate customer traction for the product or service acceptable to the business offering it. For example, the scarcity and difficulty of attracting physicians to Mori to meet the demand, and the acute pain point and suffering it created, led us to create a "Cloud Doctor Model" pull model to pilot through pivoting.

Using available digital technology and open innovation platforms, villagers could tap into doctors from all over the world. Cloud Doctor would bring them to the villager's doorstep. As we developed the prototype we worked with several healthcare partners. We are also experimenting with Health Care ATM Model with Yolo Health as the healthcare provider. The villagers, the Mori Smart Village team, and Yolo are in the process of pivoting to improve and make it easier to find and use the service.

It used to be that if a business was failing, executives would get fired. During the process of developing a Smart Village, we realized something more important. If your business model does not match what's going on in the real world, it is time to fire the model. That is why it is so crucial when companies first start to build products and services that they do so incrementally to keep their burn rate low. When the hypotheses these companies have been proven wrong, they can quickly and easily pivot to find an acceptable model for all stakeholders.

The result of these business models is "Reverse Innovation," a term that broadly refers to the process in which goods, developed as inexpensive models to meet the needs of the developing countries, are then repackaged as innovative low-cost products for more developed nations.

Increasingly Villages will become the primary source of innovation for business ecosystems as information and knowledge flow in and out through open innovation platforms. A perfect example is GE. The company developed $400 portable ECG machine to replace $250,000 machine. The original high-cost machine had a 400-page manual. It needed to be operated by highly trained technicians. The machine was linked to a $60,000 printer that runs on electricity, a utility that is not yet readily available in Indian villages. The two units are bulky and hard to transport, and villages do not have adequate roads to carry such delicate equipment. GE innovated in India and came up with a $400 MacIndia that operates on double AA batteries, fits in a backpack and there is no manual, just an ON and OFF button, and results are uploaded to the cloud in real-time so that a doctor can access from a remote location.

Reverse Innovation created a product that is now being sold in the U.S. for ambulances responding to freeways accidents. Somewhere someone's life is being saved after a highway crash because of a product developed far away to meet the needs of a village in India.

This chapter is essential to understanding the business framework and models required to successfully develop products and services in Smart Villages. Here are some additional resources to add to your understanding of each of these key ideas:

92

- "Prototyping a Scalable Smart Village to Simultaneously Create Sustainable Development and Enterprise Growth Opportunities" (with Henry Chesbrough). *Harvard Business Review,* 2017.

- "HCL's Digital Open Innovation: Enhancing Business Model Effectiveness through Talent and Customer Acquisition, Development, and Retention." *Harvard Business Review,* 2015.

- "Smart Village Ecosystems. An Open Innovation Approach" (with Henry Chesbrough). White Paper prepared for Bill Gates. Posted on https://www.linkedin.com/in/solomondarwin/

- "Strategizing open innovation: How middle managers work with performance indicators" (with Jan A. Pfister and Sarah L. Jack). *Scandinavian Journal of Management,* 2017.

- "Community Outreach Clinics: Sustainability, Schooling Dental Students and Overcoming Oral Health Inequalities" (with Anirudha Agnihotry, Solomon Darwin, Michele G. Daly, Chris S. Ivanoff DDS, Reena Kumar). *Journal of Dental Research,* 2015.

- Trianz. "Trianz to Support Smart Village Initiative Launched by the University of California, Berkeley in India." www.prnewswire.com.

- Sankar, K. N. Murali (20 June 2016). "Small is smart for this A.P. village" – via www.thehindu.com.

- "Prototyping a Scalable Smart Village to Simultaneously Create Sustainable Development and Enterprise Growth Opportunities." hbr.org.
- "HCL's Digital Open Innovation: Enhancing Business Model Effectiveness through Talent and Customer Acquisition, Development, and Retention." hbr.org.
- "Smart Village Ecosystems." www.slideshare.net.
- "Strategizing open innovation: How middle managers work with performance indicators." Scandinavian Journal of Management. 33 (3):139–150.1 September 2017. doi:10.1016/j. scaman.2017.06.001 – via www.sciencedirect.com.

Chapter Seven: The Enormous Untapped Smart Village Markets

A desolate land where nothing once grew turns into the bread basket of south India now feeding several hundred million people. Reason? Open Innovation at work in the 19th century. Mori is a village that is part of a region called Konasema; it is land between two large arteries of river Godavari where they meet the Bay of Bengal. Due to proximity to the sea, the soil was highly saline and was desolate as nothing grew. The land naturally became a condemned area where people of lower castes and untouchables occupied as they had no place else to go and pitch their tents.

The location was a famine and cyclone-ravaged area, and many died of starvation. In my great-grandparents time, they ate whatever naturally grew on salty soil or even the clay from the river beds. An Englishman called Arthur Cotton who was a Civil Engineer of the British government saw this region and was distressed and moved by the sight of the famished people.

Arthur sent a message to Queen Victoria that he found "liquid gold" in India, as the river Godavari turns brown as it carries a large amount of silt before falling into the Bay of Bengal. He said, "One day's flow in the Godavari River during high floods is equal to one whole year's flow in the Thames of England."

He brought in outside experts from other regions of India and drew up plans to turn this desolate land into a tropical paradise as we know it today. He employed the thousands of starving untouchables, my great grandfather being one of them, to dig hundred and thousands of canals inland from the two arteries. He had them plant coconut trees, as they grow in salty soil, and leaving a large square patch in the middle where rice would grow later. The yield of the millions of coconuts drew out the improving the soil for rice plantations.

Today this region is the rice bowl of south India. The Queen knighted Arthur for this incredible innovation and the villagers revered him as a god. His grave is the most visited grave by Indians in England. His barges, bridges, and dams are still standing. His daily care and supervision on horseback of his works helped make them lasting monuments to today. Many structures built by the Indian governments much later have already collapsed. Recently, the Indian government located his great-grandson and flew him to inaugurate a newly constructed dam to say a prayer, so it would not collapse.

These are two excellent examples of the power of imagination, seeing untapped potential and the power of scaling. Turning starving untouchables into valuable human beings whose works have helped feed the nation and making use of the valuable silt of the wasted waters of river Godavari. Arthur could see the river as a resource and asset that could feed starving millions. He did not see the Godavari as a deity worshiped for thousands of years. Arthur did one more thing that was socially responsible, he encouraged and brought in missionaries from England to serve the untouchables (the core labor force) and educate them to build their self-worth as human beings created equal to everyone else.

Hundreds and thousands of coolies (as they were called) were educated each night under large tents where meetings were held after a hard day's work of digging and building. The missionaries also started schools and hospitals in the region where none existed before. This movement greatly liberated the people in the region. Charles Whitehouse was one of those who later joined this movement who happened to save my grandmother from drowning.[13]

Like Arthur, today's corporations should be able to see India as an untapped resource, a resource that has enormous potential for scaling their products and services by building profitable, sustainable structures or ecosystems. They should be socially responsible and build people's self-worth, empower them with access to education and provide them with tools as Arthur did. This will return dividends, in the long run, making their businesses sustainable.

Villages represent an extremely large—and largely untapped—source of potential economic growth. In India. Approximately 67% of the population of 1.31 billion people live in the country's estimated 650,000 villages. On a national scale, India's economy is growing quickly. In 2014, India's Gross Domestic Product (GDP) grew by 7.24 percent, and in 2015 it grew by 7.57 percent.[14]

China, which has approximately one million villages, also has high but slowing GDP growth. In 2014, the economy expanded by 7.23 percent and in 2015 by 6.9 percent.[15]

In all, about 1.5 billion people in the world live in wealthy countries with highly developed economies. Almost 5.5 billion people live in emerging-market economies, such as China and India. The GDP of highly developed countries totals approximately $40 trillion; if GDP grows at an annual rate of 2 percent, the potential new value to businesses is approximately $.8 trillion per year. The GDP of emerging-economy countries is lower than that of the rich countries: it totals approximately $30 trillion. However, assuming even 5 percent growth means new value to businesses each year is approximately $2.25 trillion—nearly double the potential new value in rich economies.[16]

The potential for dramatically increasing the GDP and overall happiness of these countries lies in their ability to tap into the economic and social power that these villages represent. GDP of emerging nations consisting of 5.5 billion poor and represents a staggering $2.55 trillion opportunity for business enterprises, even if these countries grow at a nominal rate of 7.5 percent. For large firms to succeed, they will need to create value for the majority of the poor and go into the villages where the poor are located. Empowering the villagers with technology will enable them to create value that could be incorporated into the business models for large firms.

Access to the internet alone offers an enormous potential impact for companies. According to the Boston Consulting Group (BCG), by 2025 the number of internet users in India will approach 850 million. As many as 55% of those users will be in rural villages.[17] Again, according to BCG, "While digital influence is growing across all income classes, locations, and age groups, the impact in rural areas is

98

especially dramatic. Indeed, rural consumers may leapfrog their urban counterparts and adopt digital behaviors much more quickly. Less expensive mobile handsets, the spread of wireless data networks, and evolving consumer behaviors and preferences will drive rural penetration and usage, changing how rural consumers interact with companies and giving companies many more options for engaging with them."[18]

BCG added, "As India's consumer market continues to grow, and the factors described above take shape, companies will need to shed conventional wisdom (for example, that opportunities lie in big cities and at the bottom of the pyramid or that India is a male-dominant society) and adapt their business models to meet changing consumer needs and behaviors."[19] This is a market that is far too big to neglect or treat in the traditional ways.

The Smart Village is the most exceptional opportunity for global brands to expand into one of the largest emerging markets in the world. These communities represent an enormous, largely untapped source of potential economic growth for global corporations. In 2017, more than 899 million people living in India lived in villages. Across the world, the number was even more massive at 3.4 billion.[20]

These rural communities, empowered by digital technologies and open innovation platforms with access to global markets, represent an opportunity to use a proven business model to develop and scale low-margin high volume products and services. Products and services needed by the people living and working in these villages around the world. Smart Villages will become the primary source of innovation

99

for business ecosystems as digital technology drives information and knowledge flow in and out through these open innovation platforms.

There is another excellent reason to look at these Smart Villages as the source of innovative products and services. Called "Reverse Innovation" it is the process whereby products and services after being developed as inexpensive models to meet the needs of these Smart Villages are repackaged as innovative low-cost goods for the cities and less rural areas in the more developed nations.

Successfully entering these new markets means smart companies must pursue business models that have been proven to work in the Smart Village model. It means letting go of the old model of closed R&D development and utilizing a combination of new approaches including Open Innovation, Co-Innovation, Low Price-High Value Pricing, and a Fair Value Model. Being able to adopt and adapt the approaches that help make Mori a success from new leadership capabilities to a Smart Village business framework. This approach includes using the Triple-Helix Model as a guide to take advantage of the regulatory and financial capabilities of the governments in these countries, and the unrestricted experimentation and exploration offered by colleges and universities around the world. It also requires paying close attention to the success to the success and failures in Mori and the lessons that my team and I have learned as we developed the roadmap for villages everywhere.

Chapter Nine: Life in a Smart Village Today

The Smart Village, like technology, is an ongoing project always open to innovation and ideas. In a very real sense, the Smart Village is always getting smarter. Today the contrast between the village of Mori in the past and the Smart Village of Mori in the present is striking.

There are many ways to talk about the value of Smart Villages. Instead of providing objective analysis, it makes more sense to listen to the voices of the people from Mori. In their own words, we can hear them testify to the wonderful changes that the Smart Village has made in their lives. From an improved standard of living to a greater sense of satisfaction and happiness. As we listen, we can also hear how the business model worked to empower and support the community and provide new ideas and projects. Here are just a few of the stories.

Mrs. Kanthamma

"When life was getting too harsh, and things seemed like going out of control, a research team from Smart Villages program came to our rescue. They were conducting awareness drive on e-commerce, and that's when I got introduced to StoreKing, an application which lets you expand your business without increasing size of the shop. The Smart Village team educated us on the application and got us registered to the app.

Since I have become a StoreKing retailer, footfall has increased significantly. My business is not just limited to selling daily utilities, but I now recharge mobiles, DTH Connections, facilitate money transfers, etc. Integration of these services has increased profits.

The Smart Village Initiative is a blessing for us as it came in and understood the core of the problem and also acted wisely to solve the issues, with commitment in serving the society. I thank them from the bottom of my heart for Improving our living standards and helping us in understanding the digital world, and now we understand the inevitability of adopting the new trends to sustain & grow in the current world scenario. Without their support and effort, we would not have been able to send our son to a medical college."

Mr. Tarra Balakrishna

"Like many other residents of my village, I have worked in Hyderabad for around ten years and moved back home to start Agriculture as a main profession. The peaceful environment of Kinnerawada and my passion for agriculture led me to move back to my native place. I have always dreamt of spending my remaining life in my birthplace. I hold many loving memories of this village–it is a paradise to me.

A research team from UC Berkeley for Smart Villages program came to villages as an initiative for building people and country. The team identified real problems through their research and provided technology solutions through open innovation business models. They introduced an e-commerce company called BigHaat which provides all required and usually unavailable inputs for Agriculture.

The introduction of BigHaat proved to be a blessing for the residents of Kinnerawada. It has given relief to thousands of people who feared their inability to meet monthly needs for their families. The farmers are very happy with the platform which provides the inputs in a timely manner. Now, every farmer in our village can order desired products through any basic phone. We are all thankful to Smart Village team for implementing this application and their facilitation of the technology to farmers.

I would congratulate the Smart Village Initiative for the work that they have done in our village and thank them from the bottom of my heart for improving the agriculture in my village. Awareness drives conducted by them have made people realize that using technology systems in rural villages improves the people conscious behavior, thus leading to an increase in their level of happiness."

Mr. Satish Kumar

"One day, I visited my good friend Vishal and his family. After driving almost 45 minutes on the dusty road in intense heat with my bicycle, I was so happy to see him and his family. The excitement I felt upon seeing my friend was no match for the intense craving I had for some water, as I had forgotten my water bottle. However, my thirst would not be satiated.

I learned that day that drinking water scarcity is a major problem. I heard that a person named Chandu (Village Intern or Grama Mitra) from the Smart Village Program could help me, so I approached him seeking some help. I was introduced to a program called PRAMAMBHAM, which was being implemented by Smart Village team at that time. They explained to me the different types of support which they could give me, and I explained my ideas, requesting their help. After that, I was approached by local Mandal Directors from the Smart Village Team, who helped me in sorting out different steps for establishing a water plant.

For financial support, I was told about the Mudra Runa Mela program, which is going to be a joint program conducted by the Smart Village project and the SBI (State Bank of India.) With the help of the smart village team, we have completed documentation which shows that my business idea fulfills all given requirements to apply for a loan. To achieve this, the Smart Village team not only helped with the loan documents but also coached and mentored me to validate and perfect my business model throughout the whole process. I proudly received the principal sanction letter, and I was granted the right to establish my water plant– my first business!

The whole panchayat will soon have ongoing water supply! It will significantly reduce the water scarcity and make all people happier, including Vishal's family. My water plant produces 1,000 liters of healthy drinking water every hour, provided in 20-liter cans. So, it provides water for around 20,000 people. When compared to the
106

supplied water by the municipality, the water contains necessary minerals, and the overall process involves modern filtration techniques like carbon and UV filtration. The quality is way beyond the water supplied by the government, resulting in significant reduction of water-borne diseases."

Mr. Pipapla Sathyanarayana Raju

"For generations, my family has been in agricultural professions. Recently, there has been a shift from paddy cultivation to shrimp cultivation due to rising demand for seafood. No proper hatcheries were available in East Godavari until my family started the first practice of aquaculture in 1989. We began by cultivating Tiger prawns, a tedious process in which we hatched the seed from the Godavari River. Initially, the harvest was prosperous, and the revenue generation was growing. However, as the cultivation increased, new viruses compromised the crop. Tiger prawns become unviable, and the boom of the aquaculture bubble busted in the years 1996 and 1997. In those days, the international trade regulations forced us to sell to a small domestic market. It became difficult to make a living. What were we to do with our farms and investments? It was our livelihood.

The market boomed once again for many farmers and me because of the introduction of a new shrimp seed type called Vannamei. In the initial years from 2003 to 2005, the seed was able to adapt to our local conditions and the harvest prospered. Eventually, new viruses started attacking the crop due to lack of bio-security, effluent treatment, and unsustainable practices like excessive antibiotic usage. For farmers such as myself, shrimp mortality rate is the highest challenge. We only have limited period of 24-36 hours. Within these critical hours, we need to respond and take critical corrective actions. Otherwise, we will lose our shrimp and our livelihoods. Waiting for time-consuming lab test reports increases mortality rate due to a lack of information to make an educated decision.

To address these problems, the Smart Village Team assessed our pain points by doing research and came up with a solution for these challenges. They introduced technology from CFog which is based on IoT sensor principles. Solar powered IoT sensors were placed in my pond. It gives me mobile alert data about parameters such as pH, Temperature, Dissolved Oxygen (DO) and Ammonia which are very vital for shrimp harvesting.

Overall this reduced the harvest risk by reducing the shrimp mortality rate. Because of the technology's success, I arranged a meeting with all shrimp farmers to spread awareness. I conducted pond tours for fisheries department to check its functionality and reliability. The Government partnered with the CFog and provided subsidies to the farmers who wanted to employ the sensors. I would congratulate the Smart Village Initiative for the work that they have done in our village and thank them from the bottom of my heart."

There are many more success stories that the chapter contains. These are among the most outstanding. By employing the definition and adhering to the business framework, the results achieved by the community and the Smart Village Team in a such a short time is remarkable.

As a smart Village, Mori is the first village in India to achieve the following:

- Connected 100% of the village to the internet with optical fiber
- Attracted over 92 Silicon Valley companies and global attention
- Included as part of the work of two major California universities - Berkeley and Stanford
- Established a Co-Innovation Lab where villagers collaborate with tech firms on ideas for products and services
- Stored the medical data healthcare records of the community in the cloud
- Introduced digital tools and programs into the Mori schools including English Lessons
- Built a working satellite to be launched by NASA as part of the Mori students "Mori to the Moon" NASA project
- Developed smart technology and access to new markets for local industries - weaving, pottery
- Used digital technology and prototype programs for farmers including shrimp farming
- Produced 10 entrepreneurs starting their businesses including Haritha featured on TEDx Delhi
- Earned an Indian Green Building Gold rating as a Green Village
- Developed 90 new disruptive business models that can be used by other Smart Villages

- Represented as a Smart Village model for these achievements and more at the United Nations.

The list is not unique to Mori. It is the result of transforming one traditional struggling rural village into a Smart Village. Mori has already become the Smart Village of tomorrow and is a chance to see what can happen in the future to rural villages in India and the world.

Chapter Ten: The Smart Villages of Tomorrow

The archaeological evidence of cotton weavers and beautiful sarees in Indian villages goes back to 3000 B.C. Yet, the suicide rate of weavers is as high as farmers because it is a dying business due to lack of access to markets. Many Indians settled abroad are proud of their Indian heritage. I believe there is a hugely lucrative market for the weavers. Weavers could create new markets, and customer bases and sarees can be repurposed beyond just wearing them; as examples, sarees can be excellent products used as curtains, pillowcases, bedspreads, canopies, wall decorations, and in many other ways. I got this bright idea from my American wife, Amy, who uses sarees in all these ways.

A few years ago, I wanted to surprise my wife with something original from my village Mori. I had one of the local weavers make a saree from scratch with a design that she would like. When I presented to her, she asked me how much I paid the lady for all this beautiful work. Four hundred rupees, I said which is twice the price at the time. In dollars, it would have been around $7.00. She said that she would have gladly paid more than a $100 for it. The difference between the current low price and the higher return is the equity gap we are now trying to close. We will empower people in villages to preserve a legacy, a tradition, and a 5000-year-old artisan craft.

PayPal one of the firms that is the part of the UC Berkeley Smart Village Project is experimenting with doing this through an open innovation platform. Here is the magic of digitalization:

A customer sitting on the couch here in Silicon Valley visits the Village Digital Mall on the TV or a mobile device. She chooses a saree she likes that costs $100. Her click generates three text messages. The first to the weaver stating that the customer bought her saree and her bank account was credited with $80. The second text to the Store Platform Owner in India -- where the weaver uploaded the saree using her camera to provide a picture of the saree -- and credits $20 to his account. The third text to the DHL to pick it up from the weaver. This seamless real-time transaction does several things to empower the weaver directly cutting out all the middlemen and giving her a fair price.

Open innovation platforms like this provide many artisans and non-artisans access to global markets for their products. Open innovation platforms also enable them to purchase from these markets. As importantly, the open innovation platforms serve as the gateway to Global brands to sell their products back to the Smart Villages.

"The future is already here — it's just not very evenly distributed." William Gibson

All the changes and innovations that went into developing the Smart Village in Mori are now available for villages everywhere. Imagine if Smart Villages existed in every country, connected to each other like nodes in an enormous web of Co-Innovation, where the knowledge and know-how are openly shared, and markets are available anytime and anywhere. To begin, many obstacles must be overcome.

The most important include

- Bringing a common understanding between the different stakeholders
- Avoiding stereotyping approach – focus on need-based interventions
- Collecting of baseline data across all villages/wards
- Understanding partner strengths/weakness

For the Smart Village idea to become a reality everyone involved in that village – the villagers, the village leaders, the government and the corporations – must be looking outward in the same direction, sharing the same vision what life in the Smart Village can be like. A shared vision and common goals must exist between all the different stakeholders to bring the vision into focus and make it a reality. There must be a concerted effort – education programs, awareness campaigns, agreed upon standards, and more – than build and support this shared approach.

A big part of this work to achieve a shared vision is to avoid stereotyping the people in the village and approaching their needs without any input from them. The obstacle to overcome is to think that you know who they are in the abstract. The only approach that will work must focus on their needs and their actual voices telling everyone from the government to the corporations what their real needs are. Listening to the villagers is critical.

Another obstacle is the lack of data across all the villages to begin to get a true picture of the aggregate of life in the villages as it is today. There are too many assumptions about villages that are incorrect and anecdotal. There must be a collection of baseline data across all villages, a starting point that is an exact latitude and longitude of need and wants, hopes and dreams of the villages.

The Smart Villages requires partners since the villagers cannot make it happen on their own. The partners each bring many strengths and weaknesses to the development of a Smart Village. Understanding what those strengths and weaknesses are for each partner enables one to use the strengths and avoid the weaknesses. The obstacles are not insurmountable. Each village in every country can become a Smart Village when using a smart approach to each of these challenges.

Effective communication between all the stakeholders and the Smart Village program participants is a crucial factor to have a positive impact. Effective communication takes many forms. Sahaj e-Village Limited is a venture initiative by SREI Infrastructure Finance Limited (SIFL). They are developing programs and services to bridge the digital divide between urban and rural India under the flagship of the Government of India. Their goal is to bring to these digital services to "...all corners of the country." At present, Sahaj is operational in 23 states of India and has rolled out over 70,000 Sahaj centers across these 23 states. There are currently over 50 services ranging from financial inclusion, banking services, community-level water plant management, utility bill collection, data collection, government form submission, e-Learning, mobile top-ups, flight ticket booking, skill development, and more.

According to the Smart Village Team in India, "Sahaj has collaborated with Central and State Government for implementation of various centrally and state-sponsored schemes as Training Agency. Sahaj stores are mainly concentrated and established in towns and villages rather than cities, as internet inclusion is less in villages when compared to cities. The Smart Village Team helped potential entrepreneurs set up Sahaj stores in Mori and other villages. This helps create entrepreneurs in villages, and most importantly it will help villagers pay bills, purchase train and bus tickets, transfer money, and use the other services. The Smart Village Team helped nearly 14 entrepreneurs to start Sahaj stores in various villages. It was an answer that solved several pain points, from helping villagers start new businesses to making the transaction easier for the community.

Mr. Param Jyothi is an example. After finishing his college education, he wanted to start a business. He started asking about businesses which would not require a large amount of capital and give him a decent monthly income. In the process, he met the Smart Village Team. When the team explained about Sahaj franchise, he was very eager to start a business as the franchise only cost in only 1,150Rs

($17.68) and not too much training. With the help of the team members and Sahaj representatives, he started a business in his home village and started offering various services. It only took two weeks to submit the required documents and get approval. Now he earns around $155 to $185 (10,000 to 12,000 rupees) a month. The amount he invested in setting up the business was covered in less than a few months.

Mr. Param Jyothi told the team the following. "If I hadn't met Smart village team I would still be searching for employment or would be working in a small shop, Smart village team put faith in me and helped me when no one supported me. I am really grateful for the cooperation and guidance smart village team provided. Now I am earning a decent amount and helping my fellow villagers and living a new life", said a satisfied villager when asked about his view on Sahaj.

And one of his customers in the village added, "Previously we used to go to Mee-Seva in a neighboring village which is around 7 miles (11Km) from here to pay electricity bill, phone bill or to book tickets, Now, due to Sahaj establishment in our village, we don't have to travel anywhere."

It is also important to share the best practices and success stories between the partners. Nothing brings success like success, and the best practices and stories of wins need to be shared. In Mori for example, Ketos water company co-innovated with villages across all the AP districts to see what issues were most important to Andhra Pradesh. They wanted to imagine prototype technology that would solve the water problems AP faces.

The CEO, Meena Sankaran, came to Mori and collaborated with the Smart Village Team. She used what she learned to continue development on Ketos' extensive real-time water monitoring IoT network. Meena brought in her R&D team to produce a device to monitor the amount of water usage. The resulting product is a perfect example of reverse innovation and has been sold in Mexico, the U.S., and now in several other states in India.

Ketos is now working with the AP Government to use the product in more than 17,000 locations. While Meena was in AP, she collaborated with the leaders in Mori and other villages to listen to and list their pain points. Ketos then funded a successful prototype project to demonstrated how the water monitoring product could be successfully used.

There is also the need to enable and empower everyone through training, capacity building and resources mobilization. The Smart Team tells the story of Hemalatha, empowered through the Prarambham program aimed to promote rural entrepreneurship.

"Hemalatha is a resident of Polaki village. She has been a housewife taking care of her children all these years, even after achieving a postgraduate degree in Hindi literature. One of the main reasons she did not start her own business is the lack of support and finances. She dreamed of setting up her own business and creating a livelihood for other low-income women. Hemalatha imagined a business that focused on the production of eco-friendly, sustainable paper plates, an important need in rural villages to reduce the waste.

The initial stages of her business plan were always in her head, but there was never a direction or guide to channel her energy towards actually setting up the business. After visiting similar small-scale entrepreneurs sustainable paper plate production industries around her area, she decided to get started.

The Smart Village Team helped her develop the business plan, understand the finances, develop marketing materials and more – including finding and leasing an office - to get the business started. She attempted to get a loan on her own and approached several banks but was turned down. With the support of the team, she received the loan from the State Bank of India. She found workers who are excited to make a living and helps the village reduce litter and waste and produce an eco-friendly product. The team helped her carefully studied the importance of sustainability and how to reduce the costs of production while running her business.

The efforts and support of the Smart Village Team helped her start her own business in making her village cleaner. She is providing work to local villagers. Now, she can look forward to further growth in her sustainable paper plate manufacturing business.

Polaki is a main area of business, and there are plenty of opportunities. They are only missing a proper structure, or a mentor, to help people make the right decisions. The Smart Village Team helped them realize that dreams can be successfully pursued with knowledge and passion. This has given the people around their village the drive to learn more."

Encouraging smart and innovative interventions that produce more effective and efficient solutions is another key to the success. Security was a longstanding concern, and the Smart Village Team heard numerous stories about theft and trouble. They had an idea using cameras linked to police headquarters to monitor central places in the village where most of the problems were.

"They police and villagers told us about the trouble spots, and where to put the cameras, what problems these cameras needed to address, from petty theft to open defecation, and what kind of images and alerts they wanted sent to the police. We were also told by villagers how best to secure cameras to prevent the theft of the cameras themselves, and to which authorities to direct the video feed. The villagers wanted to feel that there was a new level of safety in Mori.

Oguri Peddhabbai is a resident of Mori. Like many other residents, he worked in the middle east gulf for around 20 years, then moved back to his village after he retired. He loved the peaceful environment and safety that every person wants at that point in his life. He always dreamed of spending his final days in Mori, since it is not just his birthplace, but he has memories of it being almost a paradise, a place distant from the vandalism, rowdiness and other kinds of problems he experienced where he had worked.

During the 20 years he was away, Mori changed immensely. The population grew from 200 to 2000 households, changed from a post office to many cyber cafes. Young people began to get addicted to alcohol, cars multiplied, and cases of road rage were observed. There were instances of theft. Fights started between young men, and obnoxious behavior was being constantly reported in public places. The Mori he had known, a place renowned for its serenity and peaceful environment, was losing its essence. Almost every day, there was a report of one problem or another.

Unaware of the changed scenario, when he first moved back to his village to live his dream of spending his final days in his birthplace, he was shocked to see the situation. It was difficult for him to accept the fact that this is the Mori in which he was born and grew up. Sleepless nights became like an everyday ritual for him. He was often the victim. It was traumatizing for him and his family to hear the yelling and shouting of drunk youth every night. He used to witness local fights, demolition of public property, loud music at night and rowdiness every day. He then became a regular complainant to the police but still, there was no end to this problem, Frequency of such incidents went on increasing. His family had a tough time when the hooligans damaged their Christmas stars. It was traumatizing for them. And it was excruciatingly painful for him to see Mori under such a negative influence.

It was not only him, but several Oguris like him were experiencing the same problems in Mori. Rash driving became a major problem. As a result, there were some fatal accidents in the village. It was getting very difficult to conduct peaceful public events; some anti-social activities and irksome behavior were commonly reported. He started questioning himself asking "Is this the tension-free life I wanted to be in?"

The Smart Villages Team came to their rescue. We installed CCTV cameras in various parts of the village as a part of their experiment. It was the best thing that ever happened to him and his family since he returned. Within the few weeks of installation, they observed a tremendous change in Mori. There was an immense reduction in the rash driving cases, and mob mentality was challenged. There was always a fear of being under surveillance which forced people to behave better in public.

Oguri began to experience peace at night as there was no disturbance by drunkards, and police had better control over such cases. People began reporting even a small nuisance that they felt was like a threat to them or their family. A sense of responsibility towards surroundings was returning. One thing that used to disturb him since moving back was the extremely high rate of open defecation which was largely eradicated using the cameras. He started feeling safer, and that the village was cleaner and healthier. The team helps Panchayat take steps towards the proper disposal of waste, and everyone in the village began to take this issue seriously. Everyone is under the impression that they will be caught as their public activities are continuously monitored.

The Smart Village Team added a final note to the story. "The installation of CCTV cameras proved to be a blessing for the residents of Mori. It has given relief to thousands of people who were distraught and afraid. The team is working with their corporate partner Tyco to improve the program by increasing the resolution to help identify people, make the cameras tamper-proof, and completely secure. The team is also exploring the opportunity to have people trained and able to maintain and repair the cameras."

Finally, there needs to be a running record of what is happening as a village moves from traditional towards smart, then onto being a Smart Village. It is critical that a real-time record is established that follows the challenges and their resolution. This is the only way to provide a record of shared accomplishments others can learn from and follow. For example, Plantix is a social media app used only by farmers to communicate and collaborate about agricultural diseases and issues. Farmers use the app to identify and find a way to get rid of agricultural pests and diseases. There is a community server through which local farmers can easily and quickly post advice and solutions for other nearby farmers. They can also reach out to farmers in other parts of the state, across India or anywhere in the world. The Smart Village team introduced the program to farmers throughout all 472 villages and held training programs for anyone who wanted to use the app.

Plantix provides a record of response to farming problems and solutions. That record is used every day by farmers all over the AP State and is a model of the way a system for recording the challenges, pain points, stories and successful solutions. It works for farming, and a similar app would be useful for many industries and businesses as well.

For the people of Andhra Pradesh to benefit from the prototype being created in Mori, scalability of the intended social and financial benefits is essential. For the public sector, a scalable prototype could eventually alleviate some of the need for policy interventions in cities and abroad, such as building millions of new housing units or assisting thousands of migrant workers. It also has the potential to strengthen economic growth in India and even help transform the entire developing world, which is home to millions of villagers.

For the private sector, scalability is equally key. The revenues from any one village are simply too low to justify the costs of investing in technology and other solutions. However, the total opportunity within India and other developing countries is potentially large. Designing a prototype that can successfully scale is therefore crucial to the private sector's participation, which is in turn crucial to the success of the smart village concept.

Chapter Eleven: The Start of the Smart Village Movement

The Smart Village Movement has begun. Open innovation platforms, such as the weaver's story described in the PayPal Platform illustration, could be employed for many artisans and non-artisan products. The Village Digital Mall being pivoted by Paypal, if successful and gains traction in collaboration with Smart Villages, could empower 250 million artisans in India by giving them access to US markets generating additional income for them. This platform has the potential to generate transaction volume over $100 million at only 10% of the market share. This will enhance the living conditions of millions of artisans in addition to generating PayPal an annual revenue of over $10 million. The artisan product alone is approximately a $1 Billion market[21]. Just imagine what else is possible with other products that could be on-boarded onto this platform. A win-win for all.

This Open Platform approach will provide them with access to global markets and afford them the ability to purchase directly from them serving as well as serving as the gateway to Global brands to sell their products. Open Innovation Platforms become the conduit through which knowledge, data, information will flow. This approach will achieve an economic equilibrium that will give "seed to the sower and bread to the eater" eliminating wasted resources, unnecessary time and generating satisfied customers in the process.

The vision must be real; the vision must be exciting; the vision must be something people can dream about.

Mori Smart Village is an evolving idea and not a location. My dream is that the learnings from Mori in India can become a viable model for Smart Villages everywhere. This is the genesis of the Smart Village Movement, the realization that although the numbers are staggering, the potential to have a prototype that works as a model for rural development is equal to the task. Smart villages are an idea whose time has come. Imagine what a world filled with Smart Villages would feel like, not only for the villagers, but the rest of the world.

We already know from the results in Mori what the impact of a Smart Village is on some of the people who live there. This chapter also asks a critical question. What are some of the more obvious global economic, political and societal impacts if all villages were to become "Smart Villages"?

Smart Villages would become the engines for business growth for tomorrow. Almost 5.5 billion people live in emerging-market economies, such as China and India. The GDP of emerging-economy countries is lower than that of the rich countries totaling approximately $3.0 trillion vs. 0.8 trillion - this is more than triple of that of rich economies that are growing at a meager 2%. This is a market that is far too big to neglect or treat in the traditional ways.[22]

126

Figure Ten: Three Trillion Dollar Opportunity

Addressing The Needs of the Many
A Three Trillion Dollar Opportunity
GDP $30T – Growth 7.5% = $2.25T   GDP $40T – Growth 2.0%= $0.8T

The Poor - 5.5 Bil   The Rich 1.5 Bil

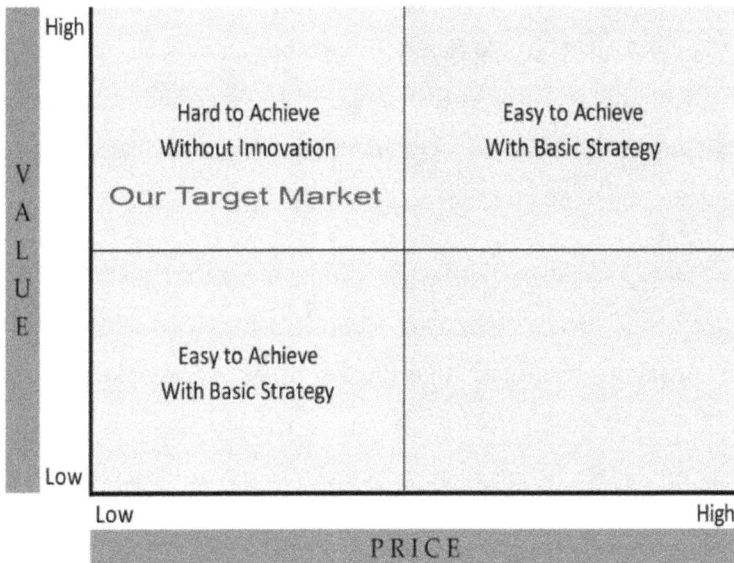

High		
	Hard to Achieve Without Innovation **Our Target Market**	Easy to Achieve With Basic Strategy
VALUE	Easy to Achieve With Basic Strategy	
Low		
	Low	High
	PRICE	

Access to the internet offers an enormous potential impact for companies. By 2025 the number of internet users in India alone will approach 850 million. As many as 55% of those users will be in rural villages. The estimate of connectivity and access worldwide by 2020 is 4.5 billion using more than 23.3 billion internet connected devices.

Cities are reaching their limits of growth and migration is unsustainable. Smart Villages can take the pressure off urban centers and provide a standard of living and level of happiness that many people in rural villages currently do not have to stem the tide of immigrants looking for opportunities to improve their lives by moving from struggling villages to cities already under pressure from unrestricted growth.

A small manageable Smart Village has already shown that it can be effectively and efficiently operated. Mori received an Indian Green Building Gold rating as a Green Village. Smart Village can bring a new environmental balance to the Earth.[23]

Smart Villages will offer the community ready access to the key "equalizers" and "empowering agents" – entrepreneurship, education, and equal opportunities. An estimated 8.1 billion people will be alive in 2025[24], the majority still living in villages in India, China, and Africa. Smart Villages represents the best way for these equalizers to become an important part of the life of the village, help the village and the villagers successfully become entrepreneurs, advance their education, and find equal opportunities as they integrate and connect to more the developed parts of the world.

There is my dream of the Smart Villages all over the world. It starts with Mori. And from that success, we can scale Smart Villages, founded on the principles and practices that make Mori work, to villages around the world

I was not born into a Smart Village, yet it was life experiences through many failures and setbacks through my journey along with the help of my colleagues and smart village team the enabled my imagination and determination to create the first successful prototype in Mori, a prototype that proves that a Smart Village is possible and can be developed everywhere.

Chapter Twelve: My Heroes - The Berkeley Smart Village Team

I knew from the start that I cannot do this alone on the ground. I needed a team that would be work like a Silicon Valley startup. The challenge was the so many came forward to join with excellent academic and professional experience, but how do you select among many those that gave me perfect answers to all my questions?

The criteria have been simple. I had to listen to their hearts as they spoke to me and chose the ones who did not ask me about a salary, were willing to give up the comforts of the city and move to a remote rural village called Mori which they never heard about. I wanted those who are teachable and could unlearn some of the things they had been taught at their universities. I looked for those who were hungry for knowledge, had a burning desire to learn something new, and attempt something that has never been done before. I wanted someone who was comfortable doing something without an instruction manual or best practices guide and not afraid to fail and keep trying and not give up until they succeeded.

I desired someone to whom I could impart all my learnings, and train and equip them to grow with me on this journey – the road to Mori was a path not traveled. I chose those who were ready to make sacrifices and who did not see this as work with any expectation but as their contribution to helping some of the most underserved people on the planet. In the end, it was a passion for the vision and commitment to the mission that I was looking for. They are all engineers from top Indian Schools, except for Werner, my former student at Berkeley, and Judah a public policy student at UC Berkeley. I want you to listen to their stories and impressions of this journey in their own words.

The stories begin with Shreya, my Smart Village Team Director in India. She graduated at the top of her class and gave up the best job offers to take on this project. A job that came with a great deal of uncertainty. She ultimately made presentations at Berkeley, Stanford, and the United Nations, making a good case for the Smart Village Movement that would serve the neglected majority.

Evani Shreya

This is the story of how I left my path of Civil Engineering, giving up building buildings and taking on building people. It all started when I was in my final year of college, and UC Berkeley came up with the Smart Cities competition in Visakhapatnam, Andhra Pradesh. That's when I first met Professor Darwin and took some lectures on Business Model Innovations and sessions on Pitching Ideas. My team won that competition and that in turn inspired me to follow Professor Darwin on LinkedIn.

Exactly a year later, Professor Darwin portrayed the vision of Smart Villages and offered for me to work on his research project in Mori. I couldn't have gotten a better opportunity. I immediately postponed my job offer and moved to the village with no clue of what was ahead except for the strong vision I shared with Professor Darwin.

132

I wholeheartedly believed in his vision from the beginning. Living in Mori was very different from how I grew up; it was exploring and building networks every day. Professor Darwin coached our team to the extent that he even taught us how to relate on personal levels with the villagers and grasp the true reality of life in Mori. The six months of the UC Berkeley Smart Village Fellowship was a great learning curve in my career.

Working at grass-root levels, helping villagers understand the importance of technology, working with corporates and giving them a complete sense of what is required to be done was my overall job as a fellow. My parents supported me fully, never did they object to me being the only girl or for living in the village for two years now. They have supported my passion as much as possible. When Phase 2 stared, I left my job because I knew we signed up for something big. Attempting Phase 2 itself was a lot of hustle with enthusiasm. Professor Darwin is a constant source of inspiration to keep going with all kinds of challenges and hurdles.

Working with the government so closely made me realize that there is so much to be done for people and our planet and that only technological solutions can fill in the gap of resources, both physical and human. This Phase brought interesting insights and experience that none of the MBA colleges could have given. I have learned to work with Corporations, Government and most importantly leading team. I thank Professor Darwin for believing in me, and for giving me these huge responsibilities with direction to make it happen. I look forward to work in this sector and pour in my efforts to build many more smart villages –a great movement Professor Darwin had started.

Werner Fischer

I am a German student who completed my Master's degree in technology. Having written a thesis on Open Innovation, I developed an admiration for Professor Henry Chesbrough, the father of Open Innovation and wanted to be his student. While exploring overseas universities offering courses that align with my vision, I came across UC Berkeley's course offered by Professor Solomon Darwin on building Smart Villages – leveraging Open Innovation. This course, aligned with my area of interest and it was a perfect fit as I always wanted to make a career in the field of sustainability of our planet.

This course changed the direction of my life. Professor Darwin is a visionary who greatly inspired me. I wished to be a part of this project because it connected every dot perfectly. Seeing my passion for this subject, he invited me to join the Smart Village project in India as director of research. I wasn't very sure initially but knew that this is something I always wanted. During this project, I was involved in Open innovation research, and I enjoyed working on-ground by bringing in companies and consulting them.

But my main part of my work has been to develop a manual and helping Professor Darwin with his second Harvard Case study that would be published by California Management Review case series at Berkeley. Gaining so much experience and tacit knowledge on this subject, I would like to continue to support and stay very involved in the most relevant movement that was started at UC Berkeley.

Harshadeep Katamaneni

When I was busy at work one day Shreya called me and asked whether I would be interested to join the Smart Village Project, for which I couldn't say no, and after a couple of hours I heard a strong voice saying "Hi, Harsha" it was professor and after talking to him I felt like I should join this project and for the first time I heard a line from him which he always says to me "Let's make it Happen" this one line from professor motivates me every day to forget all my problems and make it happen.

My family was not at all happy with my decision they didn't even talk to me for a week until I visited them personally and talked to them about the project. Everyone whom I talked to about the project felt this will not happen in India for which I just smiled at them. During this project, I worked with various agro companies and Silicon Valley startups and played an instrumental role in deploying their technology on the ground. I intend to continue adding value to my rural people in India, making the best use of the expertise I developed from this project.

Judah Darwin

I got involved in Smart Villages at the end of the Phase One. I assisted in organizing the smart village launch with the Chief Minister on December 29th, 2016. Witnessing the craze over this idea and seeing the kind of innovation and innovators that were attracted to this concept grabbed my attention. On the flight home to San Francisco, I sat next to a colleague who worked on Smart Villages. Our tickets were not coordinated, and we left Mori at separate times, but we happened to sit next to each other on the plane ride from Dubai to SFO.

I spent the entire ride discussing the opportunity that Phase Two would present to me and how I wanted to be a part of the movement.

There was one problem, I am amidst my education at UC Berkeley for Political Science. Without telling anyone, I applied for a deferral from Berkeley and to my surprise, I was granted the deferral. My mother was extremely upset with me, and my grandfather has been quite concerned that I won't continue my education. So, on May 28th, 2017 I moved from San Francisco to a small village in Andhra Pradesh, Mori.

In Mori, life deviates rashly from the life I lived in San Francisco. Common luxuries I thought were necessities were no longer available. After a month or two, I had adapted the hard way through sickness and mistakes until I was able to get into the rhythm of living in a village. Along with this, I worked hands-on with almost every project that we undertook as I was the main front for corporate relations. The logistics and intricacy of the rural world were once foreign to me even though my father hailed from the very village I was living in.

I truly had to live on the ground to acquire the authentic experience. I found myself gaining expertise in fields that I had no interest in before but quickly found attractive. I vehemently pursued several projects through which brought me a greater understanding of healthcare, education, business, politics, etc. in the village setting. Through this project, I also gained an understanding of co-innovation, open innovation, and business models. I consulted several companies on the right approach and strategy to entering the rural markets. I look forward to contributing to this movement as I continue my studies at

Berkeley and desire to participate in a big way when I did with my education at Berkeley.

Arun Sharma

I am from Delhi, my family wanted me to pursue the path that they have chosen for me. A year ago, I was all set to live my dream of becoming a professional coder at 42 Coding University in Paris, France, when I got to know about the Smart Village project through one of my acquaintances. It didn't take me a second thought about cancelling my plane ticket to pursue my higher education in Paris. I was fascinated with the vision of the project and the meaningful work Professor Solomon Darwin is doing.

During my first visit to Mori, I realized that the learnings and opportunities to grow in this project are unfettered. I had a tough time convincing my parents, getting my father's approval proved difficult. His disagreement with my decision had a debilitating effect on my morale, but my passion and admiration for this project got me here. I work here developed my professional acumen, and its benevolent mission is the whole reason for my closeness to this project. During the time here, I learnt the joy of giving back to society. During the course of this project, I worked as an open innovation researcher, consulted several multinationals on business model innovation taking advantage of my data analytics skill. The knowledge acquired throughout this project will help me bring a change, I wish to see in the world. I would love to continue bringing in sustainable development building upon the concepts of Open Innovation and Co-innovation. I would like to thank Professor Darwin for giving me an opportunity to contribute in changing lives by building people.

Venkata Krishna Kagga

I always believed that Education can alone change the life of any individual, community or even a country. After my two years of fun filled and extremely satisfying stint as a fellow in Teach For India I wanted to explore what are the other ways that I can educate people and get educated as well. This role as a research fellow of Smart Villages with Prof Darwin was an exact fit for that, where I don't just educate people on advanced technologies in various sectors but also get educated. I was asked to look after the operations of Kaikaluru Assembly Constituency. The then Health Minister was elected from here, so we've decided that I'll be taking care of Health Sector as well. The idea of the healthcare model started with the question, is it possible for the 20% of the doctors to address the needs of 72% of the Indian population that lives in rural setting? As we started interacting with villagers and local politicians we noticed the seriousness of the bad situation in the Indian health sector.

We came to an understanding that this can only be achieved by strengthening the existing system by equipping the rural healthcare workers with advanced technologies and imparting knowledge and skills needed to leverage on technological advancements from the healthcare Industry.

138

Our journey began, and it showed me what innovative ways along with technology can achieve to benefit society. Through this experience, I have learned a lot and acquired a confidence that will help me work in multiple areas of expertise. I had exclusive access to government officials and ministers which has primed my professional persona. The international attention the project brought also exposed me to several different work cultures and increased my ability to adapt according to the situations I am placed in.

I worked primarily in healthcare and through my hours of research and on the ground experiences and field visits, I have been advising the project and corporate executives on how to tackle issues plaguing Andhra Pradesh through existing channels and new innovations. Ultimately this has given me a growth spurt in professionalism and expertise that I would like to be utilized in taking this work forward to further this mission.

Lakshmi Sravani

Growing up I have experienced both sides of the coin which made me believe that empathy is as important than sympathy, so I attended different volunteer meets and took membership in few NGOs to serve the society to my best, with this continuous effort I become a team lead of an education-focused NGO named WE CAN. After completing my graduation, I thought of taking up courses in the Development management. But fortunately, I came to know that the Berkeley Andhra Smart village's project is hiring young graduates who had the passion to serve the villages. I was very much attracted by the JD and I start researching about the project then I came to know few interesting points that Mori is the first smart village in Andhra Pradesh and this was achieved under the leadership of visionary leader Professor Solomon Darwin in Phase 1 who was born in the same village. I felt that this is the best job and the best fit with the expertise I had. Initially, I applied for a post of Mandal Director.

After a short wait, I received two interview calls from Smart Villages team and cleared the first two rounds. I was invited to Mori for the final round of Interviews. I was happy at that point and made plans to visit Mori in next few weeks for the final round. All of a sudden around 7:00 pm in the evening I received a call from Smart Villages team saying that I had been selected as a core team member and if I want to take the opportunity I needed to be in Mori (which is 300 km far away) by 3:00 am the next morning. I was anxious because it was so sudden and I did not even know how to reach Mori at that late hour. Plus my parents were not comfortable sending me to Mori that late. By some way or another I convinced my parents and started to Mori, catching the last bus that night.

After all these struggles, I made it to Mori by 3:00 am in the morning, and I was warmly received by the Smart Village team when they picked me up from the bus. This one random and unexpected incident changed my whole life. I work with various government officials, elected officials and district magistrates in showcasing various educational systems for learning. I was working with Silicon Valley and Indian start-ups that have great offerings. I found through pivoting exercises that both kids and adults learn fast with access to digital tools. In the future, I would like to contribute my time and knowledge in developing digital education systems in my country with
140

all the experience I have acquired from my work at Smart Village project.

Shavan Michael Y.

While working for India's biggest e-commerce company, Flipkart as an Executive, I realized that I needed to do something more meaningful in life. When Professor Darwin invited me to work with him for Smart Villages, it was a very easy decision for me to quit my job and join this revolution. Any project needs the passion and perseverance of its participants to succeed. I see myself as a great match for the project. I am a curious, persistent and dependable person who is eager to broaden his horizons and devote a reasonable amount of time to the work. I am optimistic that the project will benefit from my contributions as much as I will benefit from the project. I also believe in a simple principle described by Professor Darwin called "Time Bound and People Bound' – Really Makes Things Happen!"

Through this incredible journey, I have discovered that I have been living in a closet for too long because this experience has opened a new world to me. I was put in the leadership position for East Godavari and closely worked with the East Godavari Collector. I managed a team of young innovators who are eager to implement technologies in villages. I also worked for the safety and security vertical in the project and was the go-to man for logistics and local expertise on the subject as well as for the project. This experience has built up a confidence in me to consult and advise people. I have lived my life receiving from people, and now I can give what I have for my community.

Teja R P

I had been working as a manager in a corporate job for a few years after my graduation. Day in and day out, everything was corporate, and I was simply unsatisfied with the 9-5 culture I was living in. I had to find something better to do with my life. One day my best friend, Prashanth, called me while I was on my way from Vizag to Hyderabad with just 50 kilometers left of a 600-kilometer journey. He explained about UC Berkeley Smart Villages project which he just started to volunteer at I pulled over a side of the road to listen to him carefully. I was very impressed with the Idea of how this innovative approach could reprise my motivation. I turned around and drove all the way back towards the east coast of Andhra Pradesh to make the interview. Following a location on Google Maps, I started to Mori. I followed the digital maps towards this job and never looked back.

At first, I worked to organize a Hackathon that had to be UC Berkeley caliber. I coordinated with 400 students to bring together young, innovative minds so that together we could tackle issues that the rural world faces. After the hackathon was over, I worked on a concept called Professional Development Center which attempts to reach rural, uneducated youth to learn a vocational trade and find job placement. I juggled 19 different corporations to make this successful. We then handed over this center to the government so that they can take the initiative forward. Now I work as a District Coordinator making sure we have ground implementation, data collection, and good relations with local leaders. These jobs have given me a vast
142

collection of experiences each teaching me new skills. More importantly, these jobs have taught me adaptability and how to innovate truly, and I look forward to contributing to this work in the future.

Rajasekhar Malireddy

I am a programmer and coder and had many opportunities in cities to work in very lucrative positions. With the budding knowledge, I worked my whole final year of engineering for the AP GOVT under the category of the internship. After this internship works, I got introduced to Smart village team due to because of the talent that I had in the aspects of Web site development and app development on DATA analysis. Upon meeting the smart village team and seeing their level of energy and passion toward this great project, I decided to join. My interactions with Professor Darwin when we were at the initial step of the smart village made me more enthusiastic about of this project. I decided to move from a city to the Mori village that felt like no sacrifice at all as I was with a great team which made all the difference.

Being a part of the Smart Village team, I have developed an official website for the project, conducted many surveys for Research also created the dashboard of the project analysis of the surveyed data. Designed a village footprint for all the 472 villages. The work experiences made me build several applications for the rural people. I have learned so many things beyond programming like business model innovation concepts and learning how start-ups and mature

143

companies think. By working on this project, I have gained the confidence to help in social welfare related projects which I desire to do with my life to help people

Afterword

When I used to lecture all over the world about Smart Cities, following my lecture too many concerns were raised and not much excitement and it drained me. However, now as I talk about Smart Villages, to different groups, from academics, corporate executives, startups, and government leaders, they all come out of the woodwork with excitement and ask me how they can contribute and join this movement. This is a movement I find that resonates in the hearts of men and women around the world. Building Smart Cities is important to enhance GDP of nations, but building Smart Villages is far more empowering and transforming. Mori has shown me that the 3.4 billion people around the world in the rapidly emerging nations, empowered by digital technologies and open innovation platforms with access to global markets, are ready to take their place in the connected world of the 21st century.

Acknowledgments

To the Enablers and Inspirers of the Smart Village Movement

I would like to thank the key government leaders in India who paved the way for getting this movement started: Vice President Venkaiah Naidu, Prime Minister Narendra Modi, Chief Minister Chandrababu Naidu and the former President of India, Pranab Mukherjee. Prime Minister Modi opened the door for my students and me at UC Berkeley to develop smart city frameworks for Ajmer, Allahabad & Visakhapatnam, in furtherance of the commitment made by Leaders of India and the United States in September 2014.

The finished frameworks were presented on May 20, 2015, to the Minister of Urban Development Venkaiah Naidu, who said that UC Berkeley should do a more in-depth study on the city of Visakhapatnam. The following year on January 10, 2016, my students and I had the opportunity to present our work in India to Chief Minister Chandrababu Naidu who was much impressed by our work and encouraged me to focus our efforts on developing models for Smart Villages, instead, where 70% of his people live.

I am grateful to Chief Minister Naidu for his guidance and support to the Berkeley-Andhra Smart Village project. My team is most inspired by his relentless efforts to uplift rural people from their misery through innovative technologies. The Berkeley-Andhra Project would not have been possible without his involvement and commissioned me to undertake the assignment.

147

I also drew much inspiration from my three encounters with the former President Pranab Mukherjee. In March 2016, I proposed establishing Smart Villages simultaneously along with cities at his innovation roundtable. The ideas were well received and applauded by everyone at the roundtable. It was at this table discussion and exchange where many of my ideas were formulated and later validated by my colleague Professor Henry Chesbrough at Berkeley. Following the President's roundtable presentation and validation, I undertook the project offered by the Chief Minister Chandrababu Naidu.

My team and I are most appreciative to Chief Minister Naidu for his guidance and support to the Berkeley-Andhra Smart Village project. My team is most inspired by his relentless efforts to uplift rural people from their misery through innovative technologies. The Berkeley-Andhra Project would not have been possible without his involvement and commissioned me to undertake the assignment. My team on the ground received tremendous support from Minister Nara Lokesh who took time to understand our roadblocks and offer his leadership for the best way forward. Rajsekhar Budithi, IAS has played a key role and has taken his responsibility to another level, has been hands on from day one offering constructive criticism, advice, and encouragement. JA Chowdary and Hari Prasad Vemuru have helped me throughout and were a constant helping hand.

VIjayanand, IAS, Babu A ,IAS and Girija Sankar, IAS has given my team enough guidance and director to work with the system. P.S. Pradyumna, the previous principal secretary to the Chief Minister and the current District Collector for Chittoor has always been a supportive friend for this project. Kartikeya Misra, District Collector for East

Godavari has been most encouraging and helpful in this project with his advice. District Collectors K. Dhanunjay Reddy, Bhaskar Katamneni, B.Lakshmikantham, from Srikakulam, West Godavari, and Krishna districts respectfully have also been fully supportive throughout the project.

Local MLAs, RDOs, MDOs and village heads have been very supportive throughout. Our team consists of over 550 people living in villages in the areas of our work. I would like to appreciate the Mandal Directors that deal with all local politics, issues, and pain points and have gracefully executed our projects.

I would like to express my gratitude to:

Professor Henry Chesbrough, the father of Open Innovation, UC Berkeley, Haas School of Business, for his support and encouragement in writing this book and converting this closed-minded accounting professor into an Open Innovation evangelist.

My Berkeley-Andhra smart village team in India and here at Garwood for their dedication to me and their passion for the Smart Village Movement: Evani Shreya, Werner Fischer, Harshdeep Katamaneni, K.V Krishna, R.P Teja, Sravani Patnala, Y.S Michael, Arun Sharma Judah Darwin and Malireddy Rajasekhar.

Daniel Schulman, CEO of PayPal, who is fully committed to financial inclusion for underserved people in the world and democratization of financial services to make the movement of money, simple, accessible, secure, and affordable. His mission has a direct impact on those to whom this book is dedicated.

Bill Gates, Co-chairperson of the Bill & Melinda Gates Foundation, for his efforts in on developing Indian villages into 'model villages' by initiating new technologies in fields of agriculture and sanitation.

Bill Ruh, CEO of GE Digital, for his influence on me to think about an ecosystem approach for delivering value to the end user.

Paul E. Jacobs, Chairman of Qualcomm, whose mission is to provide global Internet access for everybody, particularly, to those isolated in rural and remote areas to promote economic development and well-being.

Ambassador Ashok Venkatesan, the Consul General of India, in San Francisco, for educating my student's teams who worked on Smart Cities and Smart Village projects and me. He was a frequent guest lecturer at the Haas School of Business. His passion for helping unserved people and his constant search for technological solutions to alleviate their pain greatly inspired me.

The Next Book from Solomon Darwin

My personal thoughts that introduce each chapter in this book spring from the lives of three generations of my family -- grandmother, father, and myself. The story of the journeys that each of us took -- our own roads to triumph over the torment of the untouchable caste into which we were -- are expanded in my forthcoming book "The Untouchables."

In that book, you will read about my grandmother's transformation from a scorned and "worthless" woman into a successful entrepreneur and my father's path that led him from a discarded untouchable to a successful American educator (through the surprising intervention of President Richard Nixon).

And you will read more details of my own journey, some of which I've that I've shared in these pages. You will hopefully find it to be inspiring and show you that equal opportunity really is the great equalizer, and a focus on education, perseverance, and persistence can help dreams to come true.

You can find more details at SmartVillageMovement.org

A selection from Solomon Darwin's exciting new book "The Untouchables."

I arrived on American soil on September 13, 1971 in San Francisco, brought here by my father along with my family. I did not want to leave India as I knew that I could not cope with the challenges that America, the Land of Opportunity, would bring into my life.

I felt unprepared and unqualified; and I suffered from very low self-esteem due to growing up in a segregated village as an Untouchable. I had just turned seventeen, and my level of education was at a fifth-grade level at best. I could only read and write English very poorly, and I did not know other subjects beyond that.

I only had my poor schooling from a village school, where I was not taught much for many years. It was demoralizing to be the oldest boy from the remote village of Mori, India, now sitting in a city school in America. The fact that I could not make the minimum marks to advance to the next grade added to my stress. This consistent failure very early in my life due to the lack of self-worth had me thinking to end my life and resulted in one failed suicide attempt.

Since my early childhood, I was separated from my parents and was raised by my grandmother in the village of Mori until the age of eight. I was sent to a segregated school for the lowest caste, a simple thatched hut with no walls, located in the center of my village.

All grades were taught under one roof with no textbooks, notebooks, or slates. We were told to write the Indian alphabet in the sand with our fingers. I learned nothing beyond the alphabet until I was eight-years-old. Most of the time, the teacher did not show up; and when he did come, he came to pass the time rather than actually teach.

I did not enjoy school. I remember as a child grieving for my mother, who left me when I was two. She lived in a Communist Camp in a town far away to learn the sewing trade because my father enrolled her to support me while he was off to college. I do not remember knowing my father as a young child but was informed by my mother that he was suffering from tuberculosis in Vizag and may not live long.

I was depressed most of the time even though my grandmother loved me and cared for me since I was a baby. I am told that I would frequently ask people around me if the birds and other animals that came by our home had a mommy. When my grandmother took me to the Mori market, I was grieved by seeing the many little children, my age, begging for food and money – many were handicapped and had sores and bodily injuries. I used to ask my grandmother about where their mother was and what happened to them.

I faced discrimination as a little boy, being birthed into a caste which I did not and would not choose. We had a baby calf that was birthed right in front me. I eagerly watched as it came out of the womb. It became my friend and I was in love with it. It knew who I was, and I had fun chasing it around; sometimes we ran into rice fields that belong to the landlords adjacent to our home.

153

I heard screams and uproar claiming that, as a low caste, I was contaminating their land by walking on it, especially at the temple property on the corner of the intersection. They used to chase me away and said that they would kill my calf if I did it again. I was deeply affected by my fear of the neighbors immediately adjacent to me.

Once in a blue moon, I would be informed that my mom would be coming the next day to visit me. I was overjoyed, and I remember staying awake all night anxiously waiting for the sun to rise. I remember standing on the veranda that overlooked the rice fields and waiting for her to appear at the end of the narrow path that connected to the main road.

Once I saw her, I used to run as fast as my little bare feet could carry me, ignoring the many thorns that pricked my feet along the way. I was always out of breath when I finally fell into her arms. My mom cried much louder than me as we tightly embraced one another in the middle of the road. She would always bring me paisley shaped biscuits, but I refused to be comforted this way. My first words to her always upon our embrace were "Don't go away again," and she used to comfort me saying that she would stay and not go away again.

I used to hold her hand tight and lead her back to our home to show off my mom to everyone. I was so happy that she was back, and these were the happiest moments in my life. However, by late afternoon, she would disappear suddenly. I used to go in search for my mom house to house, trying to find her with so much anguish.

After many hours, when the night came, someone would tell me that she left in secret as she could not bring herself to say goodbye to

154

me. I would always inquire as to when she would return and always heard the devastating answer "not return for a while". This news would throw me into a deep depression for many days despite the love and comfort from my grandmother.

This pattern of my mother coming and leaving happened many times. I grew weary, and it was devastating for me as a child. I lost desire and hope to live.

My grandmother, Subbamma, was the only source of comfort to me during that time. She often held me and cried with me for hours and she would ask me to pray that my father may not die and that my mother would return. I was the apple of her eye, always with her; and we cuddled at night in the same cot.

However, I wanted my mother and nothing else would fill that deep longing. I loved my mom. She was a beautiful young lady, and I later found that she was only fourteen when she conceived me. There was so much grace about her, and I felt very secure when she was around me.

From the moment she arrived, she would start serving everyone in the home and doing chores for her mother-in-law, such as washing clothes, doing dishes, cooking, and serving food. She was the most selfless, nurturing woman I had ever known to this day. She was like a servant who cared for others around her, putting aside her own grief associated with the separation from her baby and dying husband.

It was much later when I realized that she had to obey my dying father's request to learn a trade that was being offered freely by the communist network to liberate people. Our separation was not a

155

choice but a necessity for her to learn skills in order to support us, so we could survive after my father would be gone.

I do not know how my deep longing for my mother ever developed and when that bond was established. However, the vacuum in my heart and the longing for my mom could not be quenched. At a later stage in my life, I resolved in my mind that I was built this way by my Maker; it was my genetic disposition.

I observe the same bond in my youngest daughter who cannot live without her mom. She latches onto her and cuddles her as she lays down to sleep at night. My son, Judah, was no different. Growing up, he would always seek me out and always wanted to be held. He would cuddle me tight throughout the church service even until he was eight-years-old when he became too heavy for me to carry.

I was teaching in France one summer when Judah was only two. My wife, Amy, brought him to the university that day. He saw me at the end of the long hallway and came running up to me as fast as his feet could carry him with his hands raised to be picked up. When we embraced, I shed a few tears for the baby I once was and grieved for that baby back in Mori cherishing the precious relationship with his mom.

To Be Continued …

Appendices

1. The Smart Village Roadmap

Executive Summary

The bottom of the wealth pyramid offers a huge untapped growth opportunity for global businesses to expand markets. However, it represents the poorest socio-economic group on earth. In India, 70% of its people live in its 650,000 villages. Suffering from an array of pain points, the rural population in emerging economies needs empowerment and access to digital tools, resources and information to become economically self-reliant. UC Berkeley's research initiative is focused on addressing these challenges through creating scalable, sustainable smart villages. According to Professor Solomon Darwin, "A smart village is a community empowered by digital technologies and open innovation platforms to access global markets".

Global brands seeking growth cannot ignore the emerging economies that are growing at over 10% GDP representing 5.5 billion people vs 1.5 billion in rich nations growing only at 2% GDP. However, this requires new business models based on scale and Open Innovation Ecosystems. The UC Berkeley project therefore facilitates and consults global brands to let them tap into rural markets with immense growth opportunities. Resulting products or services are benefitting the bottom of the wealth pyramid as these are empowering people when directly solving their prevalent pain points. The objective

157

is to provide holistic solutions to rural populations in the areas of health, education, agriculture, security, transportation, energy, communication and entrepreneurship.

In the summer of 2016, UC Berkeley was appointed by the Chief Minister of Andhra Pradesh, Shri Nara Chandrababu Naidu, as the State's research partner to offer possible solutions through a scalable smart village project. 472 villages are serving as open innovation laboratories on ground where over 500 assigned smart village fellows are exchanging with village communities, conducting relevant research surveys and are co-innovating with the rural population and national and international companies to develop the right solution for existing pain points. This approach relies on global and local firms working together to form a business ecosystem to address the needs in the most efficient and beneficiary way.

Providing an iterative prototyping process with feedback-based results from ongoing research on business model viability and from face-to-face interactions with future customers, aspiring partner firms are able to develop scalable and sustainable models by changing and adapting their prevalent business models to rural markets. However, scaling these models in emerging rural markets requires support from public and private sector. Collaborations with government, companies and start-ups are therefore facilitated by the Smart Village project. Ultimately, relevant innovative and disruptive products and services, which can directly address existing pain points, are empowering people in rural villages to enhance their happiness. Furthermore, the UC Berkeley Smart Village initiative has established a village

158

accelerator program to foster rural entrepreneurship as well as skill development centers to provide unemployed youth access to relevant education for placement.

Consequently, the overall entrepreneurial approach of the smart village project to empower people is critical when compared to traditional approaches such as government aid programs that help villagers in the short term but lack the foundation for sustainable economic development.

The UC Berkeley research initiative on building smart villages in emerging economies involves:

1. Co-creation of Open Innovation business models with over 60 national (Indian) and international companies and start-ups
2. Introduction of global brands such as Google, Techmahindra and SAP to the Andhra Pradesh Government resulting in private-public collaborations for state wide scaling efforts
3. Facilitating and bringing in direct foreign investment of $5 million to rural areas of Andhra Pradesh, India
4. Establishment of 5 Professional Development Centers to foster rural skill development for better placement
5. Publishing smart village research in the Harvard Business Review and presentation of latest research to key philanthropists like Bill Gates
6. Development of a Village Footprint Tool to make rural markets understandable for private, public and non-government sector

7. Coaching, mentoring and loan facilitation for rural entrepreneurs (over 500 funding arrangements to this date)

8. Involving academic ideas and expertise from multiple Universities via Hackathons or lectures related to the Smart Village initiative

The following are key takeaways and learnings from UC Berkeley's Open Innovation initiative:

1. Rural populations in villages are ready to embrace digital technology to empower themselves.

2. Global brands and startups are ready to invest in rural villages to expand their markets.

3. Co-innovation approach to develop business models by engaging villagers and corporates is showing traction.

4. Open Innovation Ecosystems approach is now embraced by partnering firms as a new way to deliver value to villagers given the scale and scope.

5. Understanding and addressing rural consumer behavior and cultural differences are major success factors when developing business models for the rural market of emerging economies.

6. Government frameworks and government bureaucracy can slow down and impede innovation as well as discourage risk-taking entrepreneurship.

7. Partner companies tend to lack scaling capacities, which then requires private-, public- or non-government-sector support.

8. Cautious IP Sharing willingness when forming Open innovation ecosystems as well as limited capacity to change business models according to rural markets are hindering needed disruptive innovation.

Overall Summary:

1. Urgent need for Smart Villages for sustainable development in Emerging economies exists to pave the way for development.
2. In-depth explanation of the concept of Smart Villages to enlightening readers with the Mission and Vision. [SEP]
3. UC Berkeley's Research Project Approach describing the methodology followed for enhancement of various verticals
4. Addressing the right scope for private sector, government and academia to come together and co-innovate disruptive business models.
5. This manual gives detailed description of our Iterative prototyping process and Co-innovation methodologies employed during the course of research for the implementation of technology on-ground with some real use cases of our corporate partners.
6. New insights and learnings are showing how to succeed in developing smart villages with this entrepreneurial approach.

Our objective is building and empowering people to increase the level of happiness of rural India through Open Innovation Ecosystems. As Professor Solomon Darwin states, "Open Innovation is happening in 472 villages of India to create value for rural populations and not in the ivory towers of Silicon Valley." This entrepreneurial driven approach provides novel research findings on how to successfully empower people in need by creating smart villages in emerging economies.

1. Introduction

The chief minister of Andhra Pradesh (AP), Hon. N. Chandrababu Naidu, upon taking charge in his new position, completed a series of visits to rural villages in his state of 60 million residents. Thirty-five million of these residents live in rural areas. Chief Minister Naidu seeks to create a new policy mechanism to address the many unmet needs of his constituents in AP. In June of 2016, he decided to launch an experiment called Smart Villages in consultation with outside experts including professors from UC Berkeley's Haas School of Business that serves as a research partner to provide possible outcome-based models and solutions. According to UC Berkeley Professor Solomon Darwin, "A smart village is a community empowered by digital technologies and open innovation platforms to access global markets".

This initiative is primarily funded by private organizations, with the state government providing leadership and a supporting role. On December 2016, Phase 1 prototype was completed, in Mori Village,

Andhra Pradesh. It validated two things: 1) readiness of the villagers to embrace digital technology to empower themselves and 2) willingness of global technology firms such as Google, Cisco, IBM, and Ericsson, among other corporate partners to invest in prototyping business model experiments in India. The Garwood Center for Corporate Innovation at UC Berkeley's Haas School of Business was appointed as a research partner for the Andhra Pradesh Government.

The objective of this experiment is to implement Open Innovation at the grassroots level in order to devise and deliver affordable digital technologies that rural villagers want and are willing to pay for. These affordable technologies must then be embedded in new business models that technology suppliers can scale and sustain throughout Andhra Pradesh, and later, all of India. Scalability is something that India offers to these industry partners, given its 650,000 villages where 70% of its 1.3 billion people live.[25]

Rural villagers had an overwhelmingly positive response to the successful Phase 1 prototype of smart villages. Given the success of Phase 1, Minister Naidu requested UC Berkeley to pursue 472 villages as laboratories of innovation. The Phase 2 goal is to explore and create new business models where industry partners can scale and prosper through providing value to the poor, rural population.

The initiative began in the summer of 2016 in Mori village. To date, more than 40 companies from India and outside of India, have chosen to deploy staff and equipment to the village to support the goals of this project.

2. List of Companies Engaged with Smart Village Team

	Corporations	Value Proposition
1	Google X	Free space optics fiber internet connectivity for regions disconnected to lay cables
2	SAP	Providing access to national markets by connecting Entrepreneurs to the largest b2b trade platform and enabling rural sourcing transparency.
3	Ericsson	Connected Aquaponics and Water Grid Management IoT solutions to improve farmers yield and to optimize water distribution.
4	BigHaat	India's largest one stop digital store for agriculture inputs to facilitate accessibility for quality products and knowledge.
5	cFog	Integrated approach to aqua farming using IoT sensors, machine learning and predictive analysis to provide actionable insights to increase shrimp yield.
6	AWS - WeFarm	Sharing vital information for farmers to improve lives without access to the internet.
7	MIT Pesticide sprayer	Solution developed in MIT labs that enhances usage of pesticide reducing the consumption of pesticides and soil pollution
8	PayPal	Providing a virtual digital mall solution for villagers and farmers to display their products to access new markets and customers.
9	Tech Mahindra(Hygge)	Smart Energy Microgrid Systems for Village to improve reliability and quality of power supply.

10	SeaB Energy	Modular easily configurable and scalable waste management systems to address bio waste to provide energy, fertilizer and bio gas in return.
11	Kaneka	Transforming every household and farm into renewable energy producer and user by providing high quality solar solutions without up-front investment.
12	IBM	Precision Farming technology to monitor weather forecast and yield
13	Cisco	Digital Classrooms for e-learnings. Cisco powered units for digital learnings
14	Hitachi	AC Repair and Mechanical training to ITI Electrical passed youth.
15	Qualcomm	Fisherman Application for fishermen
16	USHA International	Facilitating Skill Development on Tailoring & Certification with a go-to market plan. Specific training on e-commerce and design trends helps to increase income for women in rural Andhra Pradesh.
17	Wipro	Unique provider of micro loans starting from Rs 1000 per day with 32 times less transaction costs. Reducing time and costs to get loans by offering this in village general stores.
18	Hella	Automotive Technician Training to facilitate job placements at OEM service centers, which enhances the income level of employed youth by above Rs. 10,000.
19	State Bank of India	Providing loans to Entrepreneurs for kick starting their businesses.
20	Tyco	Surveillance via CCTV cameras to improve safety and security of public.
21	India Stack/Village Stack	Bringing India's population into the digital age by establishing presence-less, paperless and cashless service delivery.
22	Zero Mass Water	Uses solar energy to produce drinking water from Air
23	Ninjacart	India's leading Agri Marketing platform connecting farmers directly with businesses through smart supply chain.

24	New Sun Road	Modifying energy flow through cloud based Smart Micro-grid platform to facilitate integration of renewable energy and to provide stable and reliable energy without redesigning the infrastructure.
25	Med Tel	Health portal providing telemedicine services to rural populations.
26	A3 RMT	Health ATM, through which patient can consult a doctor and few diagnoses also can be done.
27	Care Hospitals	Creating value to patients in rural areas based on Public-Private-Partnerships with local hospitals.
28	Yolo Health	Building next generation virtual healthcare technologies enabling virtual care delivery, remote patient monitoring and improving access to healthcare.
29	StoreKing	Transforming already existing small stores to digital access points for rural India.
30	LinQ	Providing access to e-commerce services for villagers.
31	Sahaj	One stop information center for financial inclusion, financial services, customer service and skill development.
32	Learn on mobile	Education Tool to teach English with real time monitoring functionality.
33	Guru G	Providing teachers with a framework to better structure lectures and curriculum to uplift teaching quality.
34	Online Tyari	Online Curriculum to prepare aspiring students for Government Jobs.
35	Choice Solution	Digitization of the relationship between schools and parents with a transparent accountable monitoring system.
36	Cosine Labs	Providing certified treatment and diagnosis to the villagers at their door steps by linking RMPs with professional doctors. Powered by GE, Philips and Medal.
37	OSSS (Oriental Skills & Safety Services)	Enhancing technical Professionals (ITI – Diploma) with vocational training for growing demand in construction and manufacturing in the state & country.

38	Agrinos	Highly effective 'Green Biofermentation Technology' products with unique Plant Growth Promoting Microbes and Biostimulants to deliver greater crop yields and crop quality.
39	Statwig	Using Internet-of-things (IoT) and Block-chain technology to provide real-time tamper-proof end-to-end tracking that identifies problems and inefficiencies agriculture supply chain.
40	Ripe.io	Provide full food supply chain transparency with block chain technology.
41	Plantix	AI-Driven Mobile Crop Advisory Application which can diagnose plant diseases, pest and nutrient deficiencies.
42	Paper Boat	Juice company using local farmer supply to provide authentic, indigenous and traditional beverages.
43	We Farm	Sharing vital information for farmers to improve lives without access to the internet.
44	R Tech Engineering	Innovative certified tree climbing solution to empower coconut industry.
45	Drona Maps	Landscape 3D Mapping with Drone and Blockchain Technology
46	Kalgudi	Open Agriculture Platform to offer needed information, advice, market access and increased yields for farmers.
47	Ketos	Provides farmers with real-time, actionable data on water usage, pressure and quality/safety through remote, continuous automated smart monitoring.
48	Ecozen	On-farm solar powered cold storage provider to offer farmers cold storage capacity on demand on rental base.
49	Thanos	Introducing Drone technology for agricultural purposes such as spraying pesticides, to increase yields and address labor dependency.
50	Wehelio	Information Centers providing access to rural people for information and online services to conduct business transactions.
51	Lal10	E-commerce platform to sell authentic handicraft products from India.

52	Healthcubed	Innovative portable device to perform 30 basic diagnosis to assist health workers and doctors when treating villagers at their homes.
53	MedTel	Health portal providing telemedicine services to rural populations.
54	Bodimetrics	Smart device to monitor basic vitals of individuals and creating digital health records.
55	IDFC	Payment solution to pay cashless with biometric authentication in rural shops.
56	SBI	Providing loans to Entrepreneurs for kick starting their businesses.
57	YrReport	Platform to report traffic violations and crimes to elevate safety and security.
58	India Stack	Bringing India's population into the digital age by establishing presence-less, paperless and cashless service delivery.
59	World Bank	Fighting poverty through sustainable solutions to provide interest free loans and grants to government for capital programs.
60	Collabera	Providing training on programming and app development to build IT professionals on IOT & BIG DATA for future jobs by giving tools & global exposure.
61	Dell	Training rural Entrepreneurs on repairing computer components and maintenance to equip youth with advanced level of hardware servicing, maintenance and repairing skills.
62	Hitachi & Johsnon Controls	Tyco & Hitachi together bring a collaborative training program on maintenance & servicing of security cameras, Electronics and Air conditioners. Creating better livelihood by upskilling youth in AC repair and electronic devices.
63	Apollo Hospitals	Making medical facilities available at local PHC or other existing facilities. Increasing the healthier living and maintaining living standards through ongoing education programs.
64	Ambuja Neotica	Training skills for affordable and better-quality home construction with new innovative methods to foster

		Entrepreneurship and giving villagers access to affordable housing.
65	Global 3D	Training on 3D printing technology for future employment needs and opportunities in a new and upcoming markets.
66	Creya	Giving a competitive edge to rural professionals in the market by complementing skill development courses through Design Thinking.
67	Hero Motors	Two-Wheeler mechanical training for unemployed youth in rural areas to generate professional workforce skilled in two wheeler mechanics.
68	C Fog	Teaching installation, servicing and maintenance for IoT related technology solutions.
69	NASA	Providing tools for school children to develop Nano Satellites that help in providing weather and other relevant data.
70	APSFL	Provides affordable Digital services like Internet, Television and Telephone services through AP Fiber Grid.
71	TATA – Nest In	Partner in providing low-cost prefabricated toilets in villages through their subsidiary, Nest-In.
72	NeuroMinders	A Norway based gamification app for school students educating them with phonetics.
73	Fujitsu	Industry-leading authentication accuracy with extremely low false rates; contactless reader device provides ease of use with virtually no physiological restriction for all users.
74	Fedex	Logistics partner in delivering products sourced from rural entrepreneurs to global markets.
75	Lumax	Provides solar street lights for rural areas.
76	ITT	Tiger Toilets provide low-cost affordable and easy to build toilets in rural India.
77	Potential	Online marketplace for Weavers to sell sarees in global markets.
78	Janalakshmi	Provides micro-finance services to the entrepreneurs who need financial support.

79	Teach India	Provides English speaking skills for the rural population to help in employability opportunities.
80	Karadipath	Create Digital Interactive textbooks to facilitate the Virtual Classroom education in Schools.
81	Abard Eleener	Preserves coconut water longer using a powder technology that is mixed into packaged coconut water.
82	IGBC	Indian Green Building Council rates villages on their green village scale. Mori was rated gold as a green village.
83	Licious	One stop fresh meat delivery shop with access to chicken, lamb, seafood, marinades, and cold cuts. It's a fresh fish platform for fisherman.
84	EVx	Platform for students and youth aspiring to create their own applications but struggle with coding.
85	Cygni	Providing off grid DC solar solutions for households. Creating entrepreneurs, increasing income, and savings for villagers.
86	Call Free	ICRS service provider to reach mass audience in a quicker way for multiple purposes.
87	Sensorex	Sensor manufacturing start up working with partners in the ecosystem enabling multiple technologies for rural setting.
88	Lingel doors and Windows	A German based company providing quality doors and windows.
89	Bovlabs	Utilizing blockchain technology to create a marketplace with peer to peer trading specifically for energy.
90	HealthTap	Healthcare interface that offers telemedicine platform and AI doctor to offer diagnostic capabilities.

The Professional Development Center	
List of Firms	
Company	Value Proposition
Hella	Automotive Technician Training to facilitate job placements at OEM service centers, which enhances the income level of employed youth by above Rs. 10,000.
OSSS	Enhancing technical Professionals (ITI – Diploma) with vocational training for growing demand in construction and manufacturing in the state & country.
USHA	Facilitating Skill Development on Tailoring & Certification with a go-to market plan. Specific training on e-commerce and design trends helps to increase income for women in rural Andhra Pradesh.
Atom	Providing training on basic programming such as Python and Java.
Collabera	Providing training on programming and app development to build IT professionals on IOT & BIG DATA for future jobs by giving tools & global exposure.
IBM	Educating on revolutionary technologies like AI & Block Chain for technology driven market demands.
Dell	Training rural Entrepreneurs on repairing computer components and maintenance to equip youth with advanced level of hardware servicing, maintenance and repairing skills.

Hitachi & Johnson Controls	Tyco & Hitachi together bring a collaborative training program on maintenance & servicing of security cameras, Electronics and Air conditioners. Creating better livelihood by upskilling youth in AC repair and electronic devices.
Ambuja Neotica	Training skills for affordable and better quality home construction with new innovative methods to foster Entrepreneurship and giving villagers access to affordable housing.
Global 3D	Training on 3D printing technology for future employment needs and opportunities in new and upcoming markets.
BigHaat/Plantix Workshops	Training on different crops and modern agricultural technologies to let farmers learn and use relevant available technologies and techniques.
Creya	Giving a competitive edge to rural professionals in the market by complementing skill development courses through Design Thinking.
Agrinos	Training on yield improvement using organic bio fertilizer technology to increase farmers' income .
Heo Motors	Two-Wheeler mechanical training for unemployed youth in rural

	areas to generate professional workforce skilled in two wheeler mechanics.
C Fog	Teaching installation, servicing and maintenance for IoT related technology solutions.
Tech Mahinrdra	Saral Rozgar platform facilitates blue collar job placement for unemployed youth. Connecting blue collar job seekers with employers by bridging information gap.
Care Hospitals	Training in primary healthcare practices & Introducing high quality medical services by skilling and reskilling local health workers in technology.
Apollo Hospitals	Making medical facilities available at local PHC or other existing facilities. Increasing the healthier living and maintaining living standards through ongoing education programs.

3. The Triple Helix Model Case Study

Innovating in Emerging Rural Markets with an Open Innovation Framework

A central part of the philosophy to pursue the idea of creating smart villages is letting the private sector tap into emerging markets in a village setting. A recent study from Price Water Corporations (2017)[26] emphasizes that in general, corporates need to enhance several critical capabilities to win in emerging markets. First, aiming for operational efficiency is crucial, which comes with flexible business strategies and efficient supply chains through technology and local partnerships. Second, Innovation capability is required to find new ways to reach untapped markets and to design localized products for consumers of emerging markets. Therefore, the respective innovation process needs to be executed in a step-wise and continuous way. Third, having go-to-market excellence is required to let companies adapt to evolving consumer trends and maturing business environments. This enables significant presence across multiple channels and price points. Furthermore, this requires new technologies or sales channels, as part of an ecosystem of partners that "includes cross-sector players, public sector entities, and social sector units"[27]. In fact, it is necessary to develop a strong organization and ecosystem with local entrepreneurship and companies. Fourth and last, the needs of people are complex, are rapidly changing and differ from region to region or village to village. Thus, companies have to be on the ground to tap fully into diverse, unpredictable markets. In the end, best practices should be cross-shared globally.[28]

The following process and framework – Open Innovation Framework for Emerging Rural Markets, executed since mid-2016, addresses all these factors and beyond. It builds on several research-based methodologies, such as open innovation, lean start up and business model canvas as well as on continuous learnings and research from ongoing practice.

Introduction to the Healthcare Case Example for Illustrating the Framework

One example of implementing the Open Innovation Framework for Emerging Rural Markets comes from the healthcare sector in rural south India. It is commonly known that there are serious problems within Indian healthcare. Reports show that the density of all doctors (allopathic, ayurvedic, homoeopathic and unani) at the national-level was only 80 doctors per 100,000 population compared to e.g. 130 in China in 2016. In fact, the doctor-patient ratio in India is at a shocking ratio of 1: 1,700. Moreover, 80% of Indian doctors are located in urban areas serving only 28% of the populace.[29] This endangers the rural areas in India drastically. An innovative way to address such disastrous conditions needs to be approached to provide adequate healthcare in the village setting. The following case shows how the Smart Village initiative successfully developed a model to overcome this situation when applying the Open Innovation Framework for Emerging Rural

176

Markets. It refers to the different respective phases and stages from the framework.

"As we started interacting with villagers and local politicians we noticed the seriousness of the bad situation in the Indian health sector. The idea of this healthcare model started with the question, is it possible for the 20% of the doctors to address the needs of 72% of the Indian population that lives in rural setting?

We came to an understanding that this can only be achieved by strengthening the existing system by equipping the rural healthcare workers with advanced technologies and imparting knowledge and skills needed to leverage on technological advancements from the healthcare Industry.

Our journey began, and it showed me what innovative ways along with technology can achieve to benefit society."

Venkata Krishna Kagga, UC Berkeley Smart Village Fellow

Exhibit 4 – Applied Open Innovation Framework developed by UC Berkeley faculty

Open Innovation Framework for Emerging Rural Markets

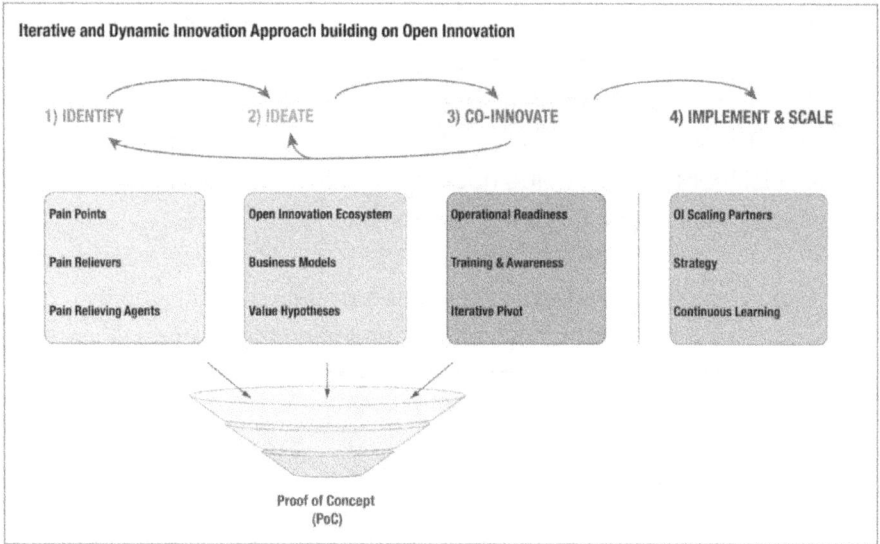

Iterative and Dynamic Innovation Approach building on Open Innovation

1) IDENTIFY   2) IDEATE   3) CO-INNOVATE   4) IMPLEMENT & SCALE

Pain Points	Open Innovation Ecosystem	Operational Readiness	OI Scaling Partners
Pain Relievers	Business Models	Training & Awareness	Strategy
Pain Relieving Agents	Value Hypotheses	Iterative Pivot	Continuous Learning

Proof of Concept
(PoC)

Phase 1:

IDENTIFY

The first phase in the Open Innovation Framework for Emerging Rural Markets comprises of identifying relevant local pain points, identifying solutions to these pain points and identifying corporations or other agents which offer specialized solutions. Within this phase, a clear sequence is not required nor recommended, as the micro and macro environment keep changing in an utmost dynamic way and all three pillars are mutually depending on each other. An iterative and dynamic process is therefore recommended.

Stage 1) Identify Pain Points

In order to identify prevalent pain points on the village level, it takes multiple efforts to obtain an objective analysis. First, incorporation of existing demographic data from e.g. the public sector helps to assess the general situation of a specific country, state and specific area. For Andhra Pradesh, the annual Socio-Economic Survey, provided by the Government of Andhra Pradesh, can present relevant insights about the general situation of the state.

Second, local government authorities are a great source of information. Merging existing research and insights with its own database is crucial to prevent redundant work. However, collected data from local bureaucrats needs to be evaluated in terms of objectiveness and correctness. Research methodologies from local sources might not fulfill quality standards or might be biased. Third, evaluating and incorporating existing national and international research on people's pain points addresses research gaps and helps to better understand the given situation. In fact, different countries often face similar problems and therefore, it is important to accumulate information and knowledge from a broad spectrum. Fourth, conducting general surveys on prevalent pain points builds the in-depth foundation of the overall research. Covering needs in different relevant sectors (see chapter Setting the scope right XY) represents the broad spectrum where innovation can improve the respective economic and social

179

situation. A general footprint survey, which covers 8 given verticals, was conducted throughout the assigned five districts of Andhra Pradesh. Over 40,000 households were asked to provide their valuable feedback about their perception regarding prevailing pain points.

Fifth, on ground community interaction gives a voice to the people to express their needs and sorrows. Continuous events in various sectors (e.g. agriculture) can give not only novel insights but also an understanding about the priority of specific needs in relation to other pain points. Community interaction is a prominent part of the smart village research to get valid and straightforward feedback.

Identifying pain points is an ongoing and essential process. It lays the foundation for all further innovation related activities. Moreover, it serves as a database for companies to ensure that their solutions meet specific pain points. The provision of in depth research about people's needs guarantees a customer centered innovation design. However, this research requires to be routine enhancement with new information to address changing behavior, evolving consumer trends and shifting complex consumer needs. Establishing such a knowledge database ultimately serves beyond enabling successful innovations in the rural sector. It can support the public sector to better frame policies and create in-depth understanding of the urgent rural needs by deriving novel research findings when applied academically.

<u>Identified Pain Points from the Case Example</u>

Identified Pain Points within the healthcare sector through surveys, official statistics and on-ground interaction.

1. Limited Access to Healthcare
    a. Village setting is characterized by 1 doctor for approximately 1,700 people (optimal: one per 400 people)
    b. Low presence of private hospitals; are located far away
    c. Inefficient process itself is time-consuming (no proper system for appointments)

2. Unaffordable high-quality Treatment
    a. Rural people cannot afford treatment from private hospitals DATA
    b. Need to rely on cost-free treatment from government hospitals, which lack quality, and unqualified rural healthcare workers DATA

3. Lack of Accountability. Risky and dangerous primary treatment by illegal health workers in the rural setting
    a. Rural Medical Practitioners (RMPs) are primary source for villagers and are not certified healthcare workers
    b. High acceptance through easy access and large availability; treatment at door step (90% presence in villages)
    c. Risky Treatment due to missing qualification and incentive to earn more money (e.g. wrong diagnosis)
    d. Missing accountability leads to repetitive or wrong treatment

Missing Quality and Efficiency in the rural Healthcare Sector in general

Conclusion: Addressing needs of primary healthcare (identified gap through research).

Rural Healthcare Worker

Several forms of health workers emerged in the village setting to compensate for the scarcity of doctors. The following are the most prominent types.

ANM (Auxiliary Nursing Midwifery): Grassroots workers in the health organization pyramid. ANMs run health Sub-centers, which are village level healthcare facilities for the community working under a Primary Health Center (PHC). Based on the population, each PHC will have 5 to 10 sub-centers. One ANM looks after 5,000 people through a sub-center. ANMs are expected to be multi-purpose health workers. ANM-related work includes maternal and child health along with family planning services, health and nutrition education, efforts for maintaining environmental sanitation, immunization for the control of communicable diseases, treatment of minor injuries, and first aid in emergencies and disasters. The provided services are cost-free as part of the Primary Healthcare, which is run by the Government in India.

ASHA (Accredited Social Health Activist): Community health workers who visit each household to advocate preventative healthcare in general and to deliver basic medicines (mostly preventive measures). ASHA workers serve mainly as a proxy for the ANMs since it is difficult for an ANM to reach 5,000 residents every day. Moreover, they ensure that patients go to the Primary Health Center (PHC) when necessary. They are mostly focused on childcare and maternal health. ASHA workers are less qualified than ANMs. Their offered service is cost-free.

RMP (Rural Medical Practitioner): People, who are practicing without a medical qualification and charging for their services. It is a violation of law as it is illegal to practice healthcare without having a license. Moreover, the abbreviation RMP actually means Registered Medical Practitioner. To hold such title, a Bachelor of Medicine and Bachelor of Surgery (MBBS) degree is required. This term evolved due to the high presence in villages to the form of Rural Medical Practitioner. To this date, Government has no clear strategy to address this issue.

Stage 2) Identify Pain Relievers

Knowing specific pain points provides detailed insights into various sectors (e.g. healthcare). It reveals gaps to be addressed. Therefore, analyzed pain relievers need to be identified with respect to innovative processes, technologies and approaches for combining several resources. Considering that innovation needs to come from a perspective of vertical innovation rather than from horizontal innovation is hereby significant. This comprises creating something new, learning from many sources and having no particular formula for innovation. By contrast, repeating what was done before and copying best practices (vertical innovation) ultimately does not lead to transformational or disruptive innovation which are required to provide high value and low-cost solutions for rural markets.

When identifying the right technologies, processes and resources, new thinking needs to be considered. In fact, this process lays the foundation for creating an open innovation ecosystem to combine and consolidate identified pain relievers for end-to-end solutions. It is critical to develop dynamic capabilities for adequately reacting to external changes and changing environments when integrating, building, and reconfiguring internal and external competencies[30]. Moreover, such abilities help to orchestrate deployment and redeployment of resources to successfully execute the innovation process. Finally, there is no defined path for identifying needed pain relievers. New thinking of horizontal innovation, where various expertise or resources from different domains can converge, new business methodologies like the open innovation paradigm and lastly, new dynamic capabilities can ultimately foster identifying the right solutions.

Identified Pain Relievers from the Case Example

To address the gap of qualified doctors in the rural setting (Primary Healthcare), new methods need to be explored. However, rural healthcare workers are already there, but qualification and experience to provide needed quality treatment is missing. Moreover, many rural health workers are illegal. The classical telemedicine approach, where

184

patients talk to doctors online, needs to be enhanced with technology and innovative processes to integrate rural health workers. High quality medical services for rural patients must to be offered with a holistic approach to address given pain points; **Access, Affordability, Accountability and Quality.** The following technologies, resources and processes were identified when considering the horizontal innovation thinking, the open innovation ecosystem methodology and the dynamic capability approach.

1) Needed innovative Technology: Digital platform to connect available doctors with patients; Technology to equip rural healthcare workers
   a) Cloud platform to efficiently connect doctors with patients
   b) Cloud platform to anchor rural healthcare workers with verified cloud physicians to provide high quality treatment at doorsteps
   c) Cloud platform to connect medical equipment to capture data and to ensure transparency
   d) Cloud platform to capture diagnosis data from the lab (excluding radiology)
   e) Portable medical equipment to do basic diagnosis and capture basic vitals

2) Needed Resources:
   a) Medical Service Provider: Lab to perform tests to provide diagnosis (with connectivity to the cloud)
   b) Human Resources: Rural healthcare workers (legal status) with decent knowledge to perform tests and execute and

communicate given advice; certified doctors to act as cloud physicians

    c) Equipment: Portable equipment (ECG), Smartphone or Computer with decent network connectivity to ensure Audio/Video consultation with the cloud physician

3) Needed Processes:

    a) Peer-to-peer process to bring together supply and demand (appointment system)

    b) Rural health workers need to be fully anchored in the system to ensure absence of mistreatments and to guarantee quality and accountability

    c) Technology equipped and anchored rural healthcare workers to provide high quality and transparent medical services at patient's doorstep (at low costs)

    d) Medical equipment to connect to the cloud platform

    e) Data capturing and electronic medical records (EMRs) created

    f) Data sharing throughout the whole process with relevant stakeholders (secondary and tertiary healthcare)

    g) Consultation, diagnosis and getting the right treatment and medicine need to be transparent and reliable

    h) Driving awareness and acceptance among the population

Stage 3) Identify Pain Relieving Agents

When aiming to identify suitable partner companies, both approaches like proactive search and leveraging the existing network can be applied. When acquiring new partner companies, certain partner criteria need to be considered to assess the suitability of collaboration within the targeted ecosystem. The smart village project acts as the facilitator and consultant for innovation activities, and organizations in such positions are acting as knowledge brokers for establishing co-innovation efforts.

For an effective collaboration process, Emden et al. (2006) identify three factors to address when aiming to collaborate for innovation: relational, technological and strategic alignment. Within compatible cultures relational alignment ensures a better conflict management and mutual alignment towards common goals (partner compatibility). Secondly, technological alignment requires unique expertise from each partner and complementary skills, resources and assets (partner expertise and partner complementary). Lastly, strategic alignment requires correspondent motivations for collaborative activities. This refers to reliability based on commitment for developing collaborative partnerships (partner reliability).[31]

Ultimately, partner criteria are critical for establishing open innovation ecosystems to tap into rural markets. Extreme conditions in the village setting require special alignment and commitment from participating companies as the overall prevalent situation is very likely to change. E.g. shifting consumer needs and consumer behavior or external alterations like policy changes. Consequently, the knowledge broker (smart village team) needs to ensure that strategic alignment is high among collaborating partners. Moreover, to guarantee the successful and efficient execution of the open innovation approach, technological alignment with respect to unique partner expertise and partner complementarity as well as relational alignment in terms of compatible partner culture are needed. Therefore, the knowledge partner has to screen potential partners with these criteria in relationship to other partners among the targeted ecosystem.

Identified Solution Providers from the Case Example

After identifying the solutions to address given pain points, several solution providers were identified. Leveraging suitable companies from the existing corporate partner network enabled bringing in latest, innovative Silicon Valley technologies (Cosine Labs). However, a proactive approach to acquire missing solution providers was needed. Therefore, several eligible companies were identified, and negotiations were started. Based on the above-mentioned criteria, GE Healthcare, Medall, Medtel and YOLO Health were selected.

- Cosine Labs
  US-based startup to provide the cloud platform (SaaS)
  Catalyst for Indian Partners (investment and consultancy)
- GE Healthcare
  Equipment provider (ECG machines) and providing digital network of cardiologists (doctors will process given information and provide this to patients'/healthcare workers)

188

- Medall Lab

  Physical Lab to do pathological tests of given samples from patients

  Cloud connectivity ensures fast delivery of the results (independent of location)

- Medtel

  IT Development to deliver all services seamlessly

- Medtel

  Cloud Physician Community of certified doctors

- Academia

  UC Berkeley and students from KIMS Hospital to consult

- YOLO Health

  Equipment provider; advice, strip-based diagnosis and medicine

Phase 2: IDEATE

Identifying pain points, pain relievers and fitting solution providers lays the foundation for ideating innovative ways to merge and consolidate given pain-relieving agents. Therefore, an open innovation ecosystem approach is applied. Moreover, the concept of shared value is implemented, where all participating actors and stakeholders are being benefited when companies not only optimize financial goals, but also social goals. Also, the concept of triple helix is part of this ideation philosophy. The triple helix concept refers to the essential inclusion of the public and private sectors along with

189

academia to provide the most efficient solution as these sectors are depending on each other.

Moreover, the process of ideating is a dynamic and iterative process. This framework builds on the lean startup approach, which continuously ensures customer centricity and concept evaluation.

Stage 1) Developing an Open Innovation Ecosystem

Creating and delivering new products, services or technologies requires business model innovation via co-development to significantly reduce R&D expenses, to expand the outputs from innovation, and to tap into new markets that have otherwise been inaccessible. Possible objectives can be to increase profitability (by lowering costs), shorten time to market (by incorporating already-developed components or subsystems), enhance innovation capability (by increasing the number and variety of front-end technologies), create greater flexibility in R&D (by risk sharing with partners) and expand market access (by broadening pathways to market for products and services). Chesbrough and Schwartz (2007) state in that context that defining such business objectives for partnering is critical for designing an open innovation business model that leverages co-development partnerships.[32] When acting as a knowledge broker, organizations (like the smart village project), which orchestrate open innovation ecosystems, need to hence clearly define the business objectives along with the participating companies from the beginning of this ideation phase.

190

In general, ecosystems tend to prevent cost aggregation and time-inefficiency for the customers since because end-to-end solutions are delivered to the customer instead of having isolated and sometimes redundant solutions. In fact, end-to-end solutions not only reduce costs and time inefficiency but also diminish complexity of operating when offering a central interface to the customer instead of multiple needed products and services. Competing companies and *complementary* industry sectors therefore converge to provide unique customer solutions. Such ecosystems are difficult to imitate, which leads to competitive advantages and a diversified product and service portfolio from individual companies when combining their expertise, knowledge and resources.[33]

Having identified solutions for given pain points and defined business objectives, it is then about ideating the aimed ecosystem by consolidating given technology, processes and resources from different actors. Despite having a crucial orchestrator and knowledge broker, participating companies need to start building relationships with each other, ideating the ecosystem design and discussing the way forward. It is crucial to design the processes collaboratively in detail for all participating actors (see case example). It is recommended that all parties co-ideate the ecosystem mutually and simultaneously. First attempts for prototypes (Minimal Viable Products[34]) and negotiations for revenue, risk and IP sharing can emerge among this early ideation phase. Such efforts can spur commitment and alignment among all participating actors to guarantee a successful project execution (see also partner criteria: partner reliability).

To ensure overall acceptance and feasibility, feedback from all stakeholders needs to be collected. Especially when innovating in the rural settings of emerging economies, it is recommended to integrate government in this ideation stage to assess the practicality of the ecosystem design with respect to legal and regulatory aspects as well as in terms of potential collaboration opportunities. Moreover, feedback from directly affected actors, e.g. service providers using co-developed solutions, needs to be collected. This can be done by tests (in case a prototype, e.g. MVP, is available) or by feedback surveys. Ultimately, response from the end consumers is critical for the overall traction and success (through e.g. surveys). In fact, applying build-measure-learn iterations as a part of the dynamic character of this open innovation framework is significant to create first ideation results. It facilitates and guarantees a process where ideas are turned into products, where consumer response is collected. It also ensures a step-wise evaluation, whether changes are needed or if continuing in the ideated way seems promising.[35]

Ideating an open innovation ecosystem is a process which takes many iterations and feedback collection efforts. It builds the foundation for the value creation for all participating actors as well as for the end-consumers. Therefore, knowledge and information gained in this stage prepares participating companies for developing their own proprietary business models and for deriving the shared value creation. Ultimately, this design needs to be turned into working prototypes to extensively test and ultimately achieve a Proof of Concept (PoC) for further implementation and scaling.

<u>Open Innovation Ecosystem from the Case Example</u>

To address given multiple pain points from primary healthcare in the rural setting, a digital platform is needed, which links all required resources (medical equipment and labs) and actors (cloud physicians, rural healthcare workers and patients) to provide a holistic solution. When equipping rural healthcare workers with portable medical equipment and anchoring them with verified cloud physicians, high quality and affordable treatment can be delivered at a patients' doorstep. Data collection and sharing throughout the whole process ensures transparency and improves the overall efficiency. Electronic Medical Records are available for relevant actors beyond primary healthcare (with patient's consent).

Providing a holistic solution for given pain points requires an Open Innovation Ecosystem approach. All identified pain relievers and respective agents, such as detected technologies, needed
resources and necessary processes from different stakeholders are therefore consolidated. The ecosystem design itself can create unique value beyond the isolated solution's value. Moreover, it accelerates the innovation process extremely when converging complementary expertise, resources and technologies.

CHANGE TO RURAL HEALTH WORKERS
Open Innovation Ecosystem Design (see Exhibit 5)
The developed ecosystem design combines and integrates the following stakeholders into a holistic system for creating shared value.

1. Customer Participation. All needed services (consultation, diagnosis, treatment and medicine) are offered under one umbrella.
2. Health Worker Participation. Equipped with digital, advanced technologies to deliver services with required quality and accountability at patient's doorstep
3. Cloud Physician Participation. Connected with the cloud platform to best utilize their time and to advise and anchor health workers with support of data.
4. Corporate Participation.
   a. Cosine Labs and Medtel collaborate to develop cloud platform
   b. GE Healthcare to provide healthcare equipment, translate analyzed data into common language (e.g. ECG)
   c. Medall as the partner for diagnosis (limited to pathological tests to this date)
5. Smart Village Participation. Central Orchestrator and Knowledge Broker. Organizing and identifying participating health workers on ground; driving public awareness
   a. Conducting Training
   b. Facilitating bureaucracy clearance
   c. Facilitating overall innovation process

The ecosystem design was co-developed and co-designed with the participating corporate partners. Their expertise and broad experience in their respective domains and fields helped to ideate this ecosystem in a lean and fast way. The smart village team acted mainly as the orchestrator within these efforts. To enable a hassle-free development

194

process, all partners agreed on general terms and conditions regarding the needed IT infrastructure. A rough draft
about economics was agreed on that all parties fully committed to move the initiative forward.

Exhibit 5 – Patient's Journey within the Healthcare Ecosystem

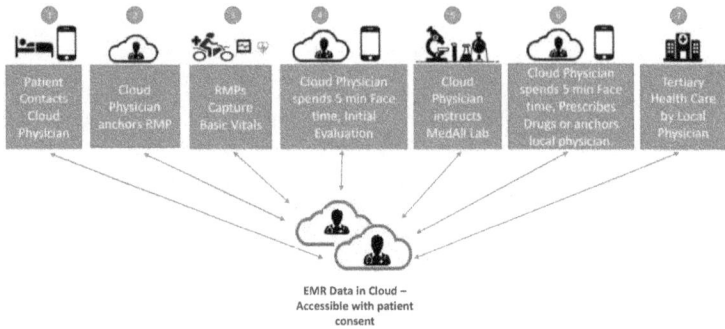

EMR Data in Cloud –
Accessible with patient
consent

Direct feedback regarding this design was collected from rural health workers and potential patients to assure first hand acceptance and demand for the model. Moreover, a general survey was conducted to validate the ecosystem design among the population of 472 villages in Andhra Pradesh. Over 7,000 data points were collected. The response was overall positive and emphasized the need and relevance for this solution. First talks with Government helped to understand their perspective on how to complement the existing system and to develop the ecosystem in a way which aligns with the legal framework and objectives from the government.

Stage 2) Business Model Development

After designing the open innovation ecosystem, every participating actor is required to develop an individual business model, which aligns with the ecosystem. However, there are critical aspects to follow. Every party needs a guarantee to sustain its own overall business model and needs to have incentives to participate in the sense of open innovation. A central orchestrator is crucial for achieving consensus, alignment and commitment among the actors. Therefore, the following steps are recommended to follow.

Classifying R&D Capabilities

When formulating effective co-development structures, required R&D capabilities need to be classified since deciding to partner externally has different implications and requires different managing approaches. Therefore, an early classification analysis needs to be performed for better developing individual business models within an open innovation ecosystem.

Exhibit 6 – Co-Development Partnerships in Relation to Required Capabilities (Chesbrough and Schwartz 2007)[36]

Partnership Attributes	Core Capabilities	Critical Capabilities	Contextual Capabilities
Partner Role	Vital; utilize in-house R&D or very select strategic partners	Important, but not core to overall business	Necessary but not value adding; develop multiple sources capability
Number of Partners	None or very few	Small number	Safety in numbers
Depth of relationship	Deep	Medium	Low
Contingency Plan	Best to develop yourself; recruit strategic R&D supplier if needed	Partner on win-win basis; align business models; go in-house only as last resort	Switch to another partner if one partner is not performing

Core capabilities refer to key sources for distinctive advantages and value creation of companies. When co-developing and leveraging these core capabilities, they need to be managed closely and shared carefully. In fact, only after an extensive strategic analysis, business enterprises should take on developing a business model which shares their core capabilities. Reducing risk can involve partnership arrangements with an equity investment or even an acquisition.

198

Critical capabilities are not about a company's core capabilities but are critical to the offered products and services. Value propositions of a company can be easily expanded when enhancing its own business with such capabilities. Business models leveraging critical capabilities therefore can create new value without investing drastically in R&D.

Contextual capabilities are able to complement a partner's core business and are not critical for its own business as these have little impact on its own value added, albeit completing the offerings. Sharing of such capabilities are very likely.[37]

Ultimately, participating companies need to assess their capabilities, which they aim to share, in terms of how critical these are for their overall success. Moreover, assessment of the other business models with respect to the different capabilities is required at the same time. Given the ecosystem design, the knowledge broker is then to orchestrate these efforts as the foundation for further business model development and the co-innovation management.

Individual Business Model Development: Optimizing the Resource Distribution

When designing the individual business models for all participating actors, the orchestrator and knowledge broker needs to ensure overall alignment & commitment from all parties for the open innovation ecosystem. Building upon the *Want, Find, Get, Manage Model* from Slowinski and Sagal (2010)[38] for executing open innovation systems, the knowledge broker along with assigned parties can optimize the distribution of resources and assets among all actors to achieve needed commitment and alignment. Therefore, from individual perspectives, the following approach is to be followed.

Central questions to be answered for orchestrating corporate partner's resources individually:

"What are the resource needs?"
"Which ones should be developed internally?"
"Which should we find externally?"

To address these questions, identified pain points and resulting pain relievers from phase 1 determined clearly what resources are needed. The ecosystem design already gives an overall picture of how the value can be delivered to the customer. To derive the particular business models for all companies, the following equation helps the central mediator to effectively balance the before defined resources individually in more detail.

Exhibit 7 – Equation for Distribution Optimization: Make/Buy/Collaborate

Fulfilled Customer Needs / Pain Points (C) = Internal Asset Base (A) + Externally Available Resources (E)

In order to meet the overall determined objective of fulfilling given pain points (**C**), the individual equation of each actor is being freed from the constraints of its own existing capabilities (**A**) through externally available resources (**E**). Due to the ecosystem design, an organizational openness is required when integrating externally available resources (**E**) and sharing internal assets (**A**). The classification of resources in terms of core, critical and contextual characteristics (see above) is crucial for this process. This equation is then to apply for each individual case and marks the start of the detailed planning process for the particular business model.

However, distributing the needed resources among the given actors requires a methodology to ensure overall efficiency and feasibility and lastly, alignment and commitment. Therefore, from each of the companies' perspectives, a Make/Buy/Collaborate decision for determined resources is be taken. This choice refers to developing assets in-house ("Make"), procuring them through traditional channels ("Buy") or partnering in the sense of open innovation ("Collaborate"). To effectively decide, it is crucial to consider the full cost of internal development, Net Present Value (NVP) . Effects of collaborating (shorter time to market or reaching the objected innovation goal more easily) and specific administrative efforts and execution challenges when collaborating. Pros and cons of sharing the resources need also to be integrated in this decision. In fact, implications of the specific resources in terms of core, critical or contextual characteristics should be assessed when resources are being shared (as explained above). A strategic analysis is hereby critical. Taking these factors into consideration, each case can be individually defined.

However, specific criteria and decision-making protocols need to be developed and applied individually, e.g. minimum requirements, assets to be complementary, transaction costs etc., which differ among various domains. Ultimately, the derived scenario needs to ensure that expected outcomes overweigh the direct and indirect costs of the collaboration.[39] Negotiations among the participating actors regarding revenue and IP sharing need to therefore continue and emerge into first drafts.

The optimization of each company's business model needs to incorporate the shared value methodology from Porter and Kramer. Taking into consideration that financial and social goals need to be met to create shared value in the long term for all stakeholders, it is critical to align with the smart village vision. Because villagers typically have very low incomes, the products and services that can both improve their lives and fit within their budgets must come at a low price and provide high value. To meet both those criteria, companies must innovate rather than rely on a basic strategy of either product differentiation or cost leadership. They must take an uncommon approach to innovating. Rather than adding new features, they must remain focused on simplicity.

For example, an electrocardiograph (ECG), a machine used to record heart activity, costs thousands of dollars and requires reliable electricity. A full-sized machine would need to be transported by truck to its destination, and it would need to be operated by a skilled technician. A highly educated cardiologist or other medical professional then interprets the results.

202

Many villages lack not just the funds to purchase such equipment for the local hospital, but also everything else necessary for the machine to serve its purpose, including easily passable roads in and out for the delivery truck. To address this need, General Electric created the MAC 400, a simplified, low-cost ECG that runs on batteries and is small enough and light enough to be portable. Since introducing the MAC 400 in 2007, GE has expanded its line of low-cost ECGs by refining the design to better meet the needs of villagers and villages. By 2011, total sales in the MAC line exceeded 10,000 units. Incorporating the shared value approach for the Indian market provided GE a good market share in India. Beyond that, they reversed innovated the low-cost product, which means offering this solution on the American sophisticated market. In the end, the product not only convinced customers in emerging markets but also in developed, heavily competitive markets.

In the end, the described process orchestrated by the knowledge broker is understood as an iterative process with all involved actors and should lead to an overall commitment and alignment for the developed business models. Moreover, evaluating the extent to which the individual business models are aligned with each other is significant to provide mutual benefits and not undercut each other.

Chesbrough and Schwartz emphasize this importance as "few companies in our experience take the time to articulate their own business model. Fewer have only clear idea about the business model of their external relationships. By assessing others' business models, understanding one's own business needs, and the degree of their alignment with one's own business model, one can turn these relationships into more valuable co-development partnerships."[40]

Framing the Business Models

After classifying particular resources and optimizing their distribution among the open innovation ecosystem, the individual business models need to be framed. The Business Model Canvas, developed by Osterwalder and Pigneur (2010)[41], provides a simplified scheme for assessing how the business is formulated in terms of value added, creation process, customer relationships and financial aspects. For the smart village initiative, Professor Darwin built upon this framework and changed it slightly for the context of emerging rural markets. It consists of eight building blocks: 1) customer segment and respective pain points, 2) value creation: what are the pain relievers?, 3) customer relationship with focus on digital relationships, 4) value distribution, 5) value capture with revenue sources and expenses, 6) needed resources which contribute to the value creation, 7) activities for value creation and which activities customers value, 8) partners to reduce risks & costs to create value. The main focus of this model lays on the characteristic of a pull business model (see exhibit 8), which combines all building blocks in the sense of open innovation when leveraging and sharing resources, expertise and knowledge. Moreover, the demand comes directly from the customer (pain point).

The Mission, vision and core values of the company or future start up need to be addressed. Goals and critical success factors define the way for succeeding with this model. To measure the progress,
204

performance metrics need to be included. Time-bound targets and the strategy then ultimately translate into an action plan for the business model execution. Lastly, the developed business models need to be evaluated to ensure ongoing customer centricity and acceptance. Therefore, feedback surveys and user tests can be conducted.

Exhibit 8 – Push and Pull Business Models

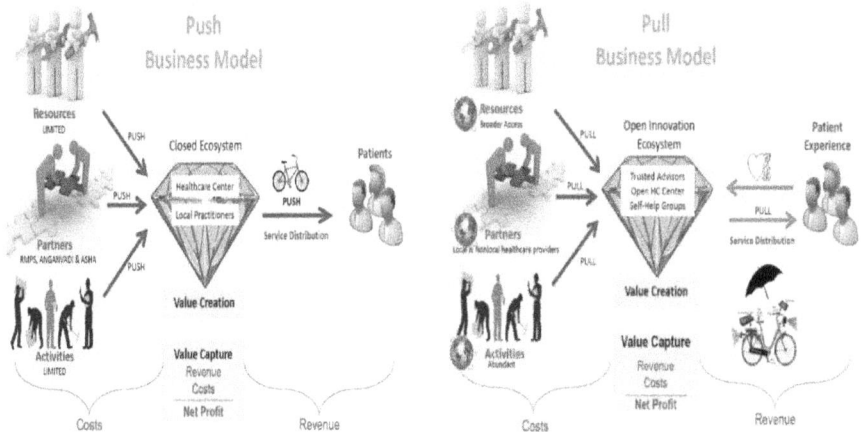

Business Models from the Case Example

After designing the ecosystem, the respective companies, the rural health workers as well as the cloud physicians needed to design their own business model within the given ecosystem. With the help of the Smart Village team and the UC Berkeley faculty as the central orchestrator, independent business models were developed. Optimal resource allocation was achieved through many iterations and negotiations (see above described methodology). The models align with the created ecosystem and with each other and give each actor monetary incentives to sustain and to further scale their participation. Critical parameters like the willingness to pay for such services or the acceptance from village population were tested in the survey with over 7,000 potential patients.

Cosine Labs

Isolated Value Creation: Providing the digital infrastructure and connecting all actors and resources to enable a seamless and data rich process.

Isolated Value Capture: As a platform owner, Cosine Labs gets small transaction commission. Co-ownership of data and IP (of the platform) with Smart Village project. Monetizing data with consent of Smart Village and customers.

GE Healthcare along with Ambient

Isolated Value Creation: Provision of healthcare equipment (GE ECG Mac 600 device and plugin device to measure blood pressure and blood saturation and oxygen) along with a customized mobile application. The application serves as the main User Interface for the rural health worker through which health workers can operate their services and patients are able access personal (historical) health data. Translation of analyzed data into common language that rural health workers can be easily processed.

206

Isolated Value Capture: Sales of equipment (along with cost free mobile application). Health workers can decide between CAPEX (investment and subscription) or OPEX (commission; pay per use) pricing model. Monetary compensation for development support is given by Cosine Labs. On average, the break-even point for an individual case is assessed to be 13 months.

Medall

Isolated Value Creation: Provides diagnosis tests from collected blood samples to the health worker and the cloud physician to advise the patient. High rural presence ensures easy logistics (30-40mn to reach the Medall labs).

Isolated Value Capture: Sales from services (analyzing blood samples).

Rural Health Worker

Isolated Value Creation: Acts as the extended hand of the cloud physician to touch and feel the patient and to execute the instruction by the cloud physician. Acts as a communicator between the patient and the doctor at patient's home.

Isolated Value Capture: Commission for every guided treatment he/she performs.

Cloud Physician (via Medtel)

Isolated Value Creation: Consultation service to provide high quality healthcare treatment remotely.

Isolated Value Capture: Commission for each consultation service.

The overall monetary distribution was negotiated multiple times throughout the whole process. Due to confidential disclosure agreements, details about revenue sharing etc. cannot be highlighted in this case example.

Stage 3) Value Hypotheses

Finalizing the individual business models among the ecosystem design leads to the necessity to formulate fundamental value hypotheses along with success KPIs before testing the model. Having applied the build-measure-learn approach continuously within the ideate phase, it is now time to build the foundation for applying this holistically to the whole model. Due to arising complexity when having an overall ecosystem design comprised of several individual business models, a clear understanding which value is to be delivered to particular stakeholders, which objectives are set and which other hypotheses need to be fulfilled, are required. Aligning with philanthropist philosophy, the pain-relieving value creation for the customers – the rural people in emerging economies, is to be derived in great detail along with specific KPIs.

In order to derive the value creation for the stakeholders and the overall fundamental value hypotheses along with success KPIs, collaborative efforts are required. All participating companies, actors and organizations as well as stakeholders, like the government, should be consulted. Ultimately, information from stakeholders, research, surveys and assumptions need to be aggregated for formulating the value hypotheses.

The derived value hypotheses are critical for further testing and implementation efforts when deriving the baseline to assess the model on. In fact, detailed success KPIs need to be determined to quantify the measurement. Moreover, it makes the concept accountable and reveals weaknesses or failures immediately. For every testing phase, an evaluation based on hypotheses ensures the broad application of the build-measure-learn methodology for fast and effective adaptation of feedback (pivoting) and effective improvements. It is recommended to incorporate digital tools for data collection and data analytics that provide data accessibility for multiple actors, which can be turned into useful information to better plan, assess and improve the progress.

Value Hypotheses from the Case Example

The given Ecosystem design is capable to provide value creation beyond the value from the isolated solutions. When targeting the needs from the rural population in terms of primary healthcare, all given pain points (**Access, Affordability, Accountability and Quality**) can be addressed. Ultimately, the ecosystem is able to create value for all participating companies, actors and organizations.

Value Creation for Stakeholders

The following value creation for each stakeholder is based on initial surveys and assumptions, derived by the participating corporate partners, the government of Andhra Pradesh and the Smart Village team along with academia. Success KPIs are hereby integrated to quantify the measurements.

1)   Value Creation for the Villager / KPIs

a)   Timely delivery of critical healthcare services

i)   Reduction of travel time (alternative to PHC since door   step delivery)

ii)   Reduction of waiting time compared to the situation at the PHC when having a proper appointment

iii)   Accelerate the service delivery time throughout the whole ecosystem (patient data sharing: electronic medical records (EMRs) now available for every relevant actor), no repetitive diagnosis from different actors in the short term

b)   Increased transparency

i)   Access to personal health history

ii)   Provision of information and knowledge to enable preventive healthcare

c)   Increased quality of treatment

i)   Certified doctors ensure reliable and accountable diagnosis with the help of the health worker

ii) Prevents wrong diagnosis because of EMR data and cloud physician

iii) Transparency through data sharing across stakeholders (with patient consent)

d) Cost reduction

i) Prevents repetitive diagnosis to save costs (and time)

ii) Reduced travel costs

iii) Open Data increases efficiency and therefore lowers costs (every dot is connected and has access)

2) Value Creation for the Cloud Physician / KPIs

a) Increased time utilization

i) Saving more lives

ii) Increasing income

iii) No need for medical infrastructure to consult remotely

b) Expanding knowledge base when practicing in rural areas remotely

3) Value Creation for the Rural Health Worker / KPIs

a) Improves work efficiency and accuracy

i) System provides information to better execute

ii) Advice from cloud physician is a continuous skill training

ii) Licensing enables social reputation and improved credibility among village communities

b) Increased monetary income

4)   Value Creation for Corporate Partners / KPIs

        a)   Improved time-to-market (open innovation)

        b)   Access to new markets when having local partners

        c)   Improving objective to save lives

        d)   Access to data from same and outside domains to improve prevalent solutions

        e)   New revenue source with this business model

5)   Value Creation for the public sector / KPIs

     a) Digital Footprint for health records in rural setting

        i)   Preventive Healthcare

        ii) Data provision supports policy making

        iii) Transparency

     b) Improved Healthcare in rural areas

        i)   Social and economic value increases

        ii) Optimizing healthcare supply chain via data driven forecasts

6)   Value Creation for Academia / KPIs

        a)   Data from rural healthcare provide new insights

        b)   International publications

        c)   KIMS college to better frame rural healthcare policies and programs when having data and research

Fundamental Value Hypotheses

The overall fundamental hypotheses for the conceptualized healthcare ecosystem represents the ideated concept in terms of ecosystem design, business models and provided value creation. The following hypotheses were used to test and assess the model among other parameters. This served to derive the baseline for the pivot (iterative test with stakeholders) to continuously improve the model.

Hypothesis 1) A scalable healthcare delivery model for rural areas is created by leveraging world-class industrial medical devices and connected care cloud infrastructure.

KPI: overall long-term success based on all KPIs

Hypothesis 2) The model is able to create collaboration among rural healthcare facilities, qualified labs and clinicians to create a self-sustaining ecosystem.

KPI: qualitative feedback from stakeholders

Hypothesis 3) All medical records are captured electronically including demographic and clinical information that can be available on demand to authorized clinicians, or government institutions.

KPI: rate of digitization

Hypothesis 4) Rural health workers are fully monitored and anchored into the system to ensure full transparency and accountability.

KPIs: rate of monitoring

Hypothesis 5) The model can provide the assumed value creation for all stakeholders.

KPIs: see value creation KPIs

Hypothesis 6) The model is adapted by patients, health workers and cloud physicians.

KPI: Adaptation Rate

Hypothesis 7) Healthcare entrepreneurship is fostered as more people start the occupation of healthcare.

KPI: long term rate derived from the number of healthcare workers

Phase 3: Co-Innovate

Ideation in collaboration with all stakeholders in the sense of open innovation merges eventually into the extensive customer centered phase of co-innovation. It is about testing and changing the designed models and defined value hypotheses with the help of villagers to eventually co-innovate self-contained and scalable solutions for existing needs. Therefore, all participating parties are required to reach their operational readiness and to develop a prototype to test the model in a broad manner on the ground. Additionally, people who are part of the solution need to be trained and awareness among rural population is to be spread. Then, the iterative testing, to evaluate whether change is needed (pivoting) can happen, to ultimately accomplish a Proof of Concept (PoC). The dynamic characteristic within this framework is dominant in this phase, to ensure adaptation in an effective manner.

214

Stage 1) Operational Readiness and Prototype

After designing the ecosystem along with individual business models and formulating success KPIs for measuring the model, operational readiness and a running prototype need to be accomplished.

All actors are required to validate the ecosystem model in the form of legal agreements, commitment and alignment. Creating a detailed action plan for the iterative test phases is hereby critical when allocating resources, IP and expertise among the ecosystem partners. A clear scope for the pivot needs to be agreed upon. Therefore, legal agreements in the form of MoUs and other formats need to be signed. The focus hereby lays clearly on the phase of iterative tests and feedback adaptation (pivot), but also should include contingency agreements to renegotiate terms and conditions after successfully achieving a Proof of Concept. Legal agreements must contain IP sharing, revenue sharing, resource sharing and overall cost sharing aspects to ensure utmost alignment and commitment for the ecosystem from all corporate partners and other parties. It depends on each individual case, which agreement is to be signed from which actors. Moreover, in some cases, legal clearance from the government is required. Therefore, agreements with local and even state level bureaucrats are to be facilitated. Ultimately, the knowledge broker, which is providing on-ground support and stakeholder facilitation (e.g. government) can be part of these legal agreements. This can particularly reduce the risk for participating companies when the orchestrator gives legal commitment to determined efforts.

Accomplishing overall validation and legal agreements, the hands-on co-innovation effort for developing a working prototype is likely to begin. In an optimal case, the co-development already started within the Ideate phase in form of MVPs (Minimal Viable Product) with first-time collected feedback, on which the companies can build on. The central knowledge broker is required to support the co-innovation process for the prototype in terms of providing advice and knowledge and orchestrating the overall co-development. It is recommended to continuously monitor the progress in terms of compliance with the determined ecosystem design, individual business models and agreed value creation (captured in the legal agreements). Lastly, before rolling out the prototype for testing in the broad scenario, feasibility tests need to be conducted to assure that no logical or technical complications will arise during the testing phase.

Operational Readiness and Prototype from the Case Example

After the ideation phase, the actors started co-innovating and co-developing a working prototype in depth to test the model. At the same time, the operational readiness was achieved to ensure the feasibility of the upcoming pivot.

Operational Readiness

To start the pivoting process, all stakeholders needed to finally validate the ecosystem model. First, a detailed scope for the pivot iterations was defined. Eventually, commitment and alignment with the co-innovation project from all participating actors was achieved in this stage of operational readiness. Therefore, MoUs, agreements and legal clearance agreements were signed.

Scope for the Pivot

Due to the illegal status, Rural Medical Practitioners (RMPs) are not included in the pivot to represent rural health worker. However, two RMPs will participate under strong surveillance from the Smart Village team to derive the potential of shifting their situation to a legal status with technology empowerment. The group of health workers will be covered by ANMs, as they are experienced, educated and have a legal status.

An appointment system will not be part of the first pivot iteration since mobile phones are not available within the target audience. Moreover, the experience of former telemedicine efforts (without diagnostics) within the Smart Village project showed, that rural residents are not familiar with an appointment system. To ensure firsthand acceptance from the patients, this system will then be implemented in the second pivot phase. Step by step adaptation is therefore ensured.

There will be a clear schedule for offering the medical services. The ANM's medical center is open to public in a designated timeframe from 9am – 3pm, where patients can come to get needed treatment. After that, a defined patient audience will be visited from the ANMs daily. This given pattern will not be changed again to ensure easy acceptance for the novel, advanced medical services from the patients.

Overall, it was planned to offer medical services to approximately X patients in Y villages by 10 AMN health workers in two iterations (each one month long). The advanced healthcare services will be offered for no cost. The corporate partners agreed to invest in this pivot to test the design and improve the solution until it reaches high acceptance, adaptation and assumed value creation.

Corporate Partners' Commitment.

After designing the ecosystem approach and the individual business model in consultation with the Smart Village project, the general value as well as the individual value creation and capturing convinced all participating companies. Results from the conducted survey validated the ecosystem model in general with data from over 7,000 potential customers. However, detailed negotiations regarding financial KPIs and sharing of intellectual property among the corporate partners were needed to agree on the required MoUs (Memorandum of Understanding) before testing the solution. A final validation from all participating companies was achieved in individual terms and conditions.

Rural Health Workers' Commitment. The Smart Village team briefed the participating Auxiliary Nursing Midwifes (ANMs) on the ecosystem model and explained the value it will bring for themselves

218

and rural healthcare in general. An agreement, which ensures no financial liability and expenses for the ANMs during the pilot was signed.

Patients' Commitment. In order to validate the overall acceptance and willingness to use such services, over 7,000 potential patients have been asked through a survey. RESULTS

Government's Commitment. In order to get approval for doing the pilot, a clear understanding about medical policies and legal terms was developed by the Smart Village team. Therefore, the elected member of a constituency (MLA) and bureaucrats (Indian Administrative Services (IAS) Officers and District Medical Health Officer) consulted the team and the corporate partners on how to move forward in terms of logistics and on how to get the required legal clearance. Given the constraint that rural medical practitioners (RMPs) have illegal status, RMPs were excluded from the pilot (besides one test case to evaluate possible solutions to verify them). Eventually, regular clearance was achieved from high bureaucrats on the district level.

Prototype

A prototype was developed collaboratively among all corporate partners. Cosine Labs took the lead and pooled in all given partners in to the development process. The Smart Village team consulted for the development in terms of addressing derived value hypotheses and ensured that the prototype can address the identified pain points. A first dry run was conducted with the Smart Village team to guarantee the functionality of all given features and the seamless process. There were multiple iterations to achieve the overall feasibility.

Stage 2) Training & Awareness

Training for participating people and spreading awareness among the public is essential before testing the ecosystem in a broad manner. Integrating novel processes, technologies and resources, and thus forming a completely new approach requires specific training. This can comprise of in depth seminars, workshops and online/video training. Educating rural people, who might lack education, literacy and technology exposure to certain extents demands sensitive and patient social interaction. In fact, miscommunication, misperception and wrong expectations can arise quickly among the participating actors. Therefore, a local team, which understands the prevalent situation and speaks the local language is recommended to support training efforts from the experts (e.g. from corporate partners).

To tackle the challenges of acceptance and adaptation of the novel solution among rural populations, awareness needs to be widely spread. Having determined the detailed scope of the upcoming test iterations (pivot), the affected villages can be individually addressed. Door-to-door awareness spreading, public gatherings with presentations, involving local media and government as well as conducting workshops are a few ways among many possibilities for creating broad awareness. It is necessary that such programs are offered for no cost to gain traction.

Ultimately, a central orchestrator is again needed for organizing and executing training and awareness programs. Having a clear understanding about the rural setting and therefore being able to guide a local team or even having a local team is a major success factor for those efforts. Moreover, the orchestrator can consult the participating companies or government in detail to effectively train rural people and to effectively spread awareness among them.

Training & Awareness from the Case Example

After achieving the operational readiness, required steps in terms of conducting training for the rural health workers and creating awareness among village population were executed.

Training

Equipping rural health workers with the latest technology required basic training. In this case, the one-week long training on provided equipment and digital tools complemented the existing medical skillset. In detail, participating health workers were trained on how to operate the given solution in different scenarios. Question and Answers sessions were repeatedly provided. In the end, it ensured that the health workers were fully understanding the process and were able to perform all needed activities to execute the designed solution.

Awareness

When introducing new innovative processes, technologies or models, the executing actors like the health workers need to be trained and beyond; awareness among the impacted population needs to be created. Acceptance and adaptation can emerge. Therefore, door-to-door presentations were being conducted to educate about the new solution, which is being tested. Additionally, awareness about preventive healthcare in general was spread to educate on the long-term impact of preventive and high-quality healthcare. Linking this to the presented solution, it strongly emphasized the individual value for potential patients (see value creation).

Stage 3) Iterative Pivot

Upon completing a first prototype, an ecosystem design, individual business models and receiving initial feedback from multiple stakeholders, it is finally time to assess if the original strategy (and hypotheses) can be persevered or whether changes are required to test new fundamental hypotheses about the model – which is called *pivoting*. Only when testing the model with real customers, with real actors executing it and finally discovering to which extent the defined and pivoted value hypotheses are true, a successful model can emerge. Building on the Lean Startup method from Eric Ries (2011) to let companies recognize the need to pivot a designed model and therefore save time and costs, a pivoting process for rural emerging markets was designed. Upon figuring out what model to test (open innovation ecosystem along with individual business models), how to measure its overall success (value hypotheses) and to figure out what product is needed (prototype), the final step is "to run that experiment and get that

222

measurement." [42] A baseline with real data can be derived and it can show whether the model is effectively on the right track or not.

Moreover, feedback collection from real customers and participating actors is then likely to highlight whether serious changes are needed. In case of required changes, existing hypotheses need to be altered and the baseline reestablished – pivoting is happening. A structured course correction is hence to be designed to test new fundamental hypotheses about the model, the product, the service, the strategy and the engine of growth. The process starts all over again. Phase 1, 2 and 3 are likely to be redone in a dynamic way to eventually change the fundamental hypotheses and to reiterate the testing. Such dynamic co-innovation efforts are utmost important to tap into rural markets which have very dynamic and niche characteristics. Ultimately, the results should show that the tests are running more productively and successfully than before. Finally, a Proof of Concept (PoC) can be achieved when showing that a determined extent of the defined and pivoted hypotheses is true – validated by real customers using it.

Exhibit Nine: The Pivoting Process

BerkeleyHaas
Haas School of Business
University of California Berkeley

Pivoting Process
Developing Technologies & Business
Models for Rural Markets

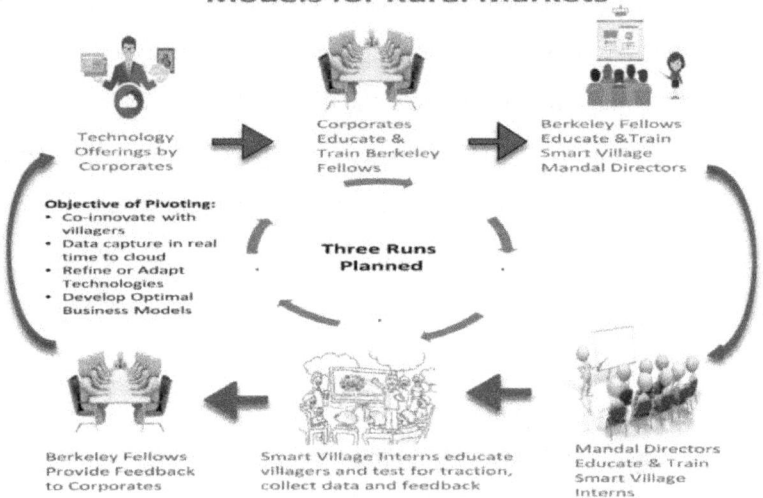

Technology Offerings by Corporates

Corporates Educate & Train Berkeley Fellows

Berkeley Fellows Educate &Train Smart Village Mandal Directors

Objective of Pivoting:
- Co-innovate with villagers
- Data capture in real time to cloud
- Refine or Adapt Technologies
- Develop Optimal Business Models

Three Runs Planned

Berkeley Fellows Provide Feedback to Corporates

Smart Village Interns educate villagers and test for traction, collect data and feedback

Mandal Directors Educate & Train Smart Village Interns

9

The pivoting process itself is designed to emphasize the co-innovation between companies and villagers to analyze and adapt profound learnings to effectively tap into rural emerging markets. Central to this process is the knowledge flow within the smart village organization (central orchestrator) to ensure high quality standards and overall success. From corporates to Berkeley fellows to Mandal Directors and lastly to Smart Village interns, everyone is required to have in depth knowledge about the designed model and its deployed technology.

224

To execute the testing of the model and to decide whether to change fundamental hypotheses (pivot), on-ground support with in depth knowledge is consequently needed. Although actors, using the novel technology e.g. rural health workers, were already trained (see stage 2), profound assistance is needed to help for the overall operations. These include inter alia logistics, technology and knowledge support, continuous training and guidance, overall orchestration and eventually the feedback collection. It is recommended that representatives from participating companies are on the ground to better understand the customer base. However, a workforce from (or lead by) a central orchestrator can cover all tasks since being experienced in the rural setting and well-educated on the model and technologies. Moreover, following the collection and analysis of the feedback after each iteration, companies are provided with recommendations on whether to persevere or change the ecosystem design, business model and implemented technologies.

The duration of a test iteration and the number of needed iterations depend on the individual requirements and the overall progress. Also, when pivoting is happening extensively, it is recommended to iterate the overall framework. Reflecting the identified pain relievers, the participating companies, the designed open innovation ecosystem along with the individual business models and lastly changing the fundamental value hypotheses along with a new test is ensuring a demanded and ready to scale solution. The orchestrator hereby plays the crucial role to be a guide and consultant for all actors. Having broad experience with such iterative processes in various domains in village settings, stakeholders can effectively and efficiently be mentored to win in rural emerging markets.

Co-Innovation Process Phase 1 in Mori

In the first stage of the smart village prototyping process in Mori, every village household was interviewed to identify the pain points shown in Exhibit 1. Interested companies then joined the project to create potential solutions.

Because people from outside the village are organizing the co-innovation process, it was important to build trust with villagers before pursuing the project further. Students from Andhra University visited each household to introduce the next stages of the project and explain how it would benefit villagers. And, because connectivity is essential for the project to work, the state government is providing fiber-optic Internet access to the village and an incentive for each household to fully participate in the prototyping process: a box that, in conjunction with a small keyboard, converts a television set into a basic personal computer.[43]

Next, a co-innovation space was built. It is a two-acre site with buildings that look similar to those already in Mori, to make the prototyping space feel like a representation of the village's future. It is in this site that the proposed technologies are displayed for villagers to view, interact with, and evaluate. All village households were invited to participate in the program, and those that participate in all three evaluation rounds will receive the connectivity box.

226

In the first round, villagers listen to a presentation about the concept of a smart village and how the evaluation process works. Then, they visit each station in the co-innovation space to learn about each proposed solution and provide feedback on the proposed features and price. They do not have to answer complicated surveys; rather, they vote using simple icons: one of a smiling face, one of a frowning face, and one of a neutral face.

Using the data collected in the first round, companies will revise their proposed solutions, which villagers will evaluate in the second round. In their third visit to the co-innovation space, villagers learn about the final solutions they will be able to purchase.

One proposed solution from IBM is intended to help farmers increase yields and decrease expenses. Sensors placed in the soil will measure the levels of water, nitrogen, and other crucial factors contributing to yields. With this information, farmers can optimize both water usage and fertilizer purchases.

Another proposed solution comes from Ericsson and is intended to monitor the gates and canals used to distribute water in the village. Sensors will be installed to measure real-time water flows. A display showing these flows will sit in Naidu's office, and farmers can provide feedback on their access to water using just their cell phones.[44]

After the third round of the prototyping evaluation in Mori, leaders from 40 nearby villages will visit Mori to learn about the proposed innovations. They will also offer feedback on how well they believe the proposed solutions will meet the needs of their communities.

The entire prototyping process is intended to facilitate the development of a self-contained sustainable business model that is scalable. To succeed, firms will have to create products and services that meet villagers' needs—as defined by villagers—at affordable prices. Those successful offerings will therefore be more likely to offer value to villagers elsewhere in the state of Andhra Pradesh, in India, and in other developing countries.

Iterative Pivot Process from the Case Example

During the ongoing ideation process, the scope for the upcoming pivot was finalized and the iterative test was ready to start.

First Iteration

10 ANMs and 2 RMPs will start the first iteration in their respective villages. The smart village team will support all ongoing activities to ensure the best possible performance. Feedback surveys which test the value hypotheses and success KPIs to derive the baseline will be conducted after 30 days.

Second Iteration

The feedback will be analyzed and handed out to the corporate partners to pivot the healthcare model. Moreover, the appointment system will be integrated and tested in the second iteration. After another 30 days, the second feedback collection will start. In the end, an advanced version of the healthcare ecosystem can be achieved when incorporating all given feedback and evaluating the model in terms of given value hypotheses and success KPIs.

Milestone: Proof of Concept (PoC)

The Proof of Concept (PoC) can be reached after proofing the fundamental hypotheses (to a defined extent) with feedback collected by all stakeholders during the iterative pivot process. Therefore, a quantified methodology needs to be followed to achieve robust results. Final quantified results with respect to the defined KPIs are compared to the baseline (and changed baseline when being pivoted) and to the desired results. An overall evaluation of the achieved result needs to be discussed with all stakeholders. The given results are then decided to be sufficient for a Proof of Concept (PoC). Otherwise, a reiteration of the 3 phases is to be considered.

Phase 4: Implement & Scale

Finally, after reaching the level of the Proof of Concept (PoC), scaling and implementation can follow. However, determining the detailed scope to which extent the model is being implemented. Based on that evaluation, it can be assessed if additional partners are required. Moreover, a strategy with specified objectives and activities linked to a compelling business scenario is to be derived in a collaborative manner. Lastly, only continuous learning and improvements are spurring long term impact on society and economy.

Stage 1) Open Innovation Scaling Partners & Scope

Having proofed the overall model in the form of a Proof of Concept (PoC) provides huge scaling potential. Therefore, a clear scope for the desired scaling initiative along with its implementation (e.g. how many villages to deploy the model) needs to be determined. However, market research about the targeted areas is critical to assure that the model is working comprehensively. When deriving that similar applicable micro and macro conditions are prevalent, respectively, relevant and needed traction can be forecasted. Consequently, when setting the scope for scaling, these factors need to be considered.

Upon setting the scope for scaling, it is necessary to assess whether existing partners within the open innovation ecosystem are sufficient for the aimed scale. A critical factor hereby is the availability of the central orchestrator for the desired scope. Not only is this orchestrator a major success factor for the overall project execution, but it is also required to provide or lead on-ground resources for training and awareness programs as well as for implementation support. In the end, the orchestrator plays a major role within all operations since having broad expertise, experience and knowledge to let companies tap into emerging markets. This is crucial to be taken into consideration, especially when lacking a central orchestrator for the aimed scaling scope. Therefore, an assessment about the potential in terms of resources, technology readiness, capabilities and strategic commitment from participating companies needs to be taken on. Moreover, valuable collaborations with the government should be evaluated since those collaborations are intended to complement and enhance efforts from both – private and public sectors mutually to certain extents (see chapter Triple Helix Theory).

230

Ultimately, when deciding to enhance or change the existing constellation of companies and organizations, further open innovation scaling partners are to be recruited in the same way as the process of identifying pain relieving agents. Since the network has significantly increased through the open innovation ecosystem, an extended corporate network can be leveraged for recruitment. Moreover, a proactive search for fitting companies can be conducted. Technological, relational and strategical alignment are hereby to be assessed to derive a successful and promising match (see Phase 2). Talks are then to be moved forward for building relationships and discussing the upcoming efforts to eventually derive a scaling strategy in the next step.

Open Innovation Scaling Partners and Scope from the Case Example

After successfully achieving a Proof of Concept (PoC) for the Healthcare Ecosystem, an assessment regarding the potential scope needs to be conducted. Therefore, the smart village team and the participating corporate partners will need to evaluate the given micro and macro situation. In the end, the scope for scaling to approximately 12,000 villages of Andhra Pradesh (to cover the majority of villages) within the next four years can be possibly determined. Potentially needed scaling partners are then to be determined, especially when considering that the smart village team is only present in 472 villages.

Moreover, the Government of Andhra Pradesh is supposed to act as a consultant partner within this assessment. When scaling into other villages, resources for conducting training and awareness efforts and for generally supporting the model need to be ensured. Moreover, it is assumed that participating companies are not sufficient to provide needed resources for the aimed scale. Consequently, the following partners could address the requirements.

Assumed Scaling Partners:

1) *Additional:* Government of Andhra Pradesh
   a) Health, Medical and Family Welfare Department
   b) Support and resource provider to be able to make the ecosystem sustainable

2) Cosine labs (IT Infrastructure in big scale)

3) Cloud Physicians (Medtel)

4) *Additional:* MedTel (Cloud Physician Platform to provide more doctors on demand)

5) Medall (Laboratories present in whole Andhra Pradesh)

6) Tricorg (Medical equipment and result-translation into easy language)

Stage 2) Scaling & Implementation Strategy

Having determined the scope of scaling along with corporate partners and organizations, strategic programs need to be co-developed among all partners as preparation for a successful strategy execution. Objectives, strategic activities, organizational structure, budgeting, resource allocation and lastly, a detailed action plan are to be determined (see also phase 2 ideate) and linked to a well-founded business case. Channels to reach the customer, pricing strategies and overall operations are to be addressed in this context.

Value creation, IP and revenue sharing are again to be defined to reach overall alignment and commitment from participating actors. Research from the World Economic Forum (2015) on collaborative innovation indicates that being open about the likelihood of failure and respective risk is crucial when defining objectives and assessing the business case for collaborative innovation projects. Incorporating these factors into broader corporate risk assessments within the business case is therefore significant.[45] Due to the dynamic characteristics of the previous pivoting phase where changes are expected and appreciated for developing suitable models, the scaling phase should be executed in a linear way and with less risk since having achieved a Proof of Concept (PoC). Hence, broad risk assessment is consequently to be executed.

Moreover, the scope of future business activities is meant to be vastly increasing compared to the pivoting phase and therefore, renegotiations and new negotiations with respect to legal agreements, objectives, activities and the overall business case are required (see also phase 3). An orchestrator in this context is crucial to ensure compliance with the overall vision about the value creation for all stakeholders in the sense of the shared value philosophy. Moreover, acting as an intermediate fosters timely negotiations and the finalization of the scaling strategy anchored to a business case. Ultimately, total consensus – on personal and legal levels is to be achieved.

In case of changing constellations within the open innovation ecosystem, it is recommended to reassess and, if necessary, change the ecosystem design along with individual business prior to developing the scaling strategy. When changing too many variables or aiming for markets with different situations (compared to the pivoted area), it is up to the risk assessment if new pivot iterations are needed or not.

After finishing the strategy, execution follows. Building solutions for the aimed scale in collaboration and in the agreed setting is to be done.

Scaling & Implementation Strategy from the Case Example

After finalizing the Proof of Concept (PoC) and determining the needed scaling partners, a scaling and implementation strategy among the corporate companies, the smart village team and the Government of Andhra Pradesh needs to be developed. The aimed objective hereby is a sustainable approach. In order to ensure overall success for implementing the healthcare ecosystem in large scale, clear objectives for the whole ecosystem which require specific activities need to be derived. Important issues with respect to the design of the organizational structure, budgeting and resource allocation among all partners need to be included. Eventually, a well-founded business case with risk assessment is required to which all scaling partners legally agree to.

Assumed clear objectives from all actors:

1) Complementing the existing healthcare ecosystem to fill the existing gaps
2) Equipping and educating rural healthcare workers with advanced technology and innovative processes
3) Increase the quality of the rural healthcare
4) Maximizing the reach of quality healthcare services to decrease the mortality rate
5) Each actor benefits from the ecosystem

Assumed strategic activities for further implementation and scaling:

1) Government to provide needed resources that ANM services remain cost free
   a) Schemes are released to cover the costs of the healthcare service
   b) Develop a new healthcare policy
2) Cosine Labs to ensure training for all participating health workers
3) ANMs and Asha workers to provide awareness for respective villages where the services are offered
4) Government to build on the developed healthcare ecosystem for legalizing RMPs
   a) Data sharing between Government and participating private companies
   b) Smart Village team to consult and orchestrate

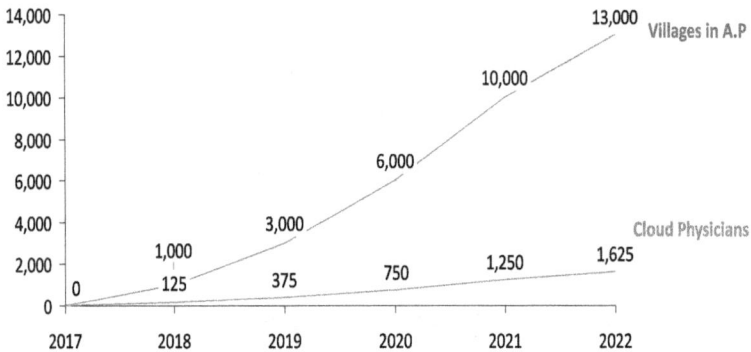

Scalable Healthcare Model

"Support Entire Rural Segment of Andhra Pradesh"

- Estimate based on 6 appointments/day/ RMP
- Team is planning to scale to 300+ doctors by end of 2018

Exhibit 10 - Potential Business Case

While the pilot covers 10 villages, scaling the consultative service model to 13,000 villages will require 1,200+ doctors, based on 6 appointments/village/day. To support a gradual build up, the targeted pace is to involve one district every quarter. The organization is planning to bring 300 doctors by itself in the system by the end of 2018 to support onboarding of 2 districts (roughly 2,000 villages). In addition, an automation of appointment scheduling and call center support are planned to enable the aimed scaling.

Alignment and Commitment: Every actor needs to commit and align with the planned execution in the large scale of the healthcare ecosystem.

Therefore, a MoU between the main actors needs to be signed. A possible approach would be a MoU between government and Cosine

236

Labs, whereas the remaining actors (Medall, Medtel) have individual MoUs/contracts with Cosine Labs.

Stage 3) Continuous Learning and Improvement

Throughout scaling and implementation activities, continuous learning and improvement is a significant part for delivering value to society, economy and business enterprises. Incorporating the build measure learn cycle from the Lean Startup approach doesn't end after achieving a Proof of Concept (PoC). Due to ever-changing micro and macro factors like consumer behavior, markets, pain points and regular frameworks, pivoting can never halt. Consequently, the ecosystem is required to evaluate regularly the prevalent situation in terms of adaptation needs. Continuous research efforts with respect to given micro and macro situations are required. Regular feedback collection from customers is especially crucial.

Following the pivoting methodology, existing value hypotheses are then to be questioned and changed and eventually to be tested in form of an (iterative) pivot. The framework cycle is to be executed again and the existing product and service needs to be adapted to these changes. Continuous learning and improvement are fostered. This ensures not only satisfaction of the customers when responsively addressing their pain points but also works as a growth engine for the ecosystem, when able to spread the solution to new areas.

It is recommended to establish such needed processes within the organization of the ecosystem model or executing these via central knowledge broker / orchestrator. Measurement leads to learning and adapted learning eventually leads to improvement with extended value creation. Following the shared value and triple helix concept along with the open innovation methodology, private sector, academia and public sector need to be continuously involved in a collaborative way to provide the best possible outcome for society and economy.

Continuous Learning and Improvement from the Case Example

Following activities need to be ensured to accomplish continuous learning and improvement for the healthcare ecosystem. (See Cloud Physician Model next page)

Exhibit 11 – Cloud Physician Healthcare Model

Cloud Physician Healthcare Model

1) IDENTIFY → 2) IDEATE → 3) CO-INNOVATE → 4) IMPLEMENT & SCALE

1) IDENTIFY

Pain Points
1) Limited Access to Healthcare
2) Unaffordable HQ Treatment
3) Lack of Accountability within rural Healthcare
4) Missing Quality and Efficiency in the Healthcare Sector in general

Pain Relievers
1) Needed Technology: Cloud Platform to connect and anchor all parties and capture data; Medical Equipment for diagnosis
2) Needed Resources: Medical Service Provider (Labs); Human Resources (Health Workers and Doctors); Equipment (Portable ECG, Smartphone, Internet Access)
3) Needed Processes: Appointments, Anchoring and Equipping Health Workers, EMRs, Data Capturing and Sharing

Pain Relieving Agents
1) Cosine Labs (Cloud Platform)
2) Tricog (Equipment Provider)
3) Medall Labs (Labs to perform tests)
4) Ambient Tech. & Coherent Med (IT Development)
5) cloudphysician.net (certified cloud doctors)

2) IDEATE

Open Innovation Ecosystem
1) Patient contacts Cloud Physician
2) Cloud Physician anchors Health Worker
3) Health Worker captures Vitals
4) Video chat with patient (Cloud Physician), initial evaluation
5) Cloud Physician instructs Lab
6) Cloud Physician gets result, prescribes drugs and anchors local Physician
7) Tertiary Healthcare by local Physician
Shared EMR Data in Cloud

Business Models
1) Cosine Labs. Platform owner, transaction based commission, Co-Ownership of Data and IP
2) Tricog along with Ambient. Sales on equipment (CAPEX & OPEX model)
3) Medall Labs. Sales from Services
4) Rural Health Worker. Commission for guided treatments
5) Cloud Physician. Commission for each consultation service

Value Hypotheses
1) Timely delivery of critical healthcare services in HQ, transparency and in a affordable way at doorsteps.
2) Improving Social Reputation of Rural Health Workers.
3) Digital Footprint for Health Records.
4) Lucrative Business for Corporates.
5) Adaptation from rural patients.
6) Fostering Healthcare Entrepreneurship

3) CO-INNOVATE

Operational Readiness
1) Pilot Scope. Excluding RMPs (illegal) and appointment system; ANMs along with ASHA workers equipped to offer services in X villages to Y patients for no costs; 2 month duration
2) Validation by all Stakeholder incl. local Government.
3) Cloudplatform with connectivity to medical equipment, cloud physician and Rural Health Worker. EMRs are created.

Training & Awareness
1) Training. Basic training on medical equipment and digital tools. Q & A sessions.
2) Awareness. Door-to-door presentations about the model and preventive healthcare

Iterative Pivot
1) Iteration. Test and feedback Collection.
2) Iteration. Feedback adaptation and second test phase.
Data collection to validate model in terms of hypotheses and KPIs.

4) IMPLEMENT & SCALE

OI Scaling Partners
1) Scaling Scope. 12,000 Villages in Andhra Pradesh in 4 years
2) Scaling Partners.
- Additional: AP Government Support and Resources
- Additional: MedTel (cloud physician)
Other partners remain.

Strategy
1) Objectives.
- Complementing rural Healthcare
- Equipping and Educating rural Health Workers
- Increasing Quality of rural Healthcare
- Each actor benefits
2) Strategic Activities:
- Government ensures cost free service provision
- Training & Awareness
- Efforts to legalize RMPs with model
- Data Sharing with Government

Continuous Learning
1) Continuous Monitoring
2) Feedback collection from health workers and patients
3) Regular strategy meetings
4) Providing data to Academia

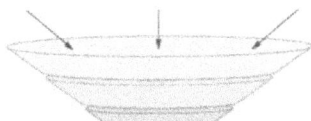

Proof of Concept (PoC)

To be determined. Value Creation and Hypotheses are proofed to be right within iterative pivots.

239

1) Continuous Monitoring from Government as well as from Cosine Labs.

2) Feedback collection from health workers and patient's Regular strategy meetings to discuss feedback and the way forward.

3) Providing data to Academia for research to get additional results and new ideas.

Notes

Chapter One: In the Beginning

[1] "Prototyping a Scalable Smart Village to Simultaneously Create Sustainable Development and Enterprise Growth Opportunities." hbr.org.

[2] "Smart Village Ecosystems. An Open Innovation Approach" (with Henry Chesbrough). White Paper prepared for Bill Gates and Hon. Chief Minister Naidu of Andhra Pradesh.

[3] *The Road to Smart Villages: An Open Innovation Approach*, Berkeley Haas School of Innovation, April 1, 2018, Professor Solomon Darwin

Chapter Two: The Inevitability of Change

[4] https://homegrown.co.in/article/8139/10-incredible-inventions-that-changed-rural-india

[5] Ibid

[6] McLuhan, Marshall. *Understanding Media*. (Gingko Press, 1964, 2003) p 6.

Chapter Six: Smart Village Business Models and Open Innovation

[7] http://facultybio.haas.berkeley.edu/faculty-list/chesbrough-henry

[8] Chesbrough, Henry William (1 March 2003). *Open Innovation: The new imperative for creating and profiting from technology*. Boston: Harvard Business School Press. ISBN 978-1578518371

[9] Ibid.

[10] https://en.wikipedia.org/wiki/Triple_helix_model_of_innovation

[11] https://en.wikipedia.org/wiki/Loet_Leydesdorff

[12] https://economictimes.indiatimes.com/industry/healthcare-biotech/80-per-cent-of-indian-doctors-located-in-urban-areas/articleshow/53774521.cms

Chapter Seven: The Enormous Untapped Smart Village Markets

[13] Source about Arthur's works: They were men sent from God: A centenary record, 1836-1936, of gospel work in India amongst Telugus in the Godavari Delta and neighboring parts Unknown Binding – 1937by Eustace B Bromley (Author)- available on Amazon.

[14] https://www.bcgperspectives.com/content/articles/center-consumer-customer-insight-marketing-changing-connected-consumer-india/
[15] Ibid.
[16] https://www.bcgperspectives.com/content/articles/center-consumer-customer-insight-marketing-changing-connected-consumer-india/
[17] Ibid.
[18] Ibid.
[19] Ibid.
[20] https://www.eventbrite.co.uk/e/healthcare-business-models-for-emerging-economies-tickets-44400238308?aff=es2

Chapter Eleven: The Start of the Smart Village Movement

[21] https://www.ibef.org/exports/handloom-industry-india.aspx - $ 100 Mio worth transactions in one year of handloom (from whole rural India to US-Markets) in 2016

https://www.omicsonline.org/open-access/the-sector-of-handicrafts-and-its-share-in-indian-economy-2223-5833-1000S3-009.php?aid=83355 - $ 870 Mio worth transactions in one year of handicrafts (from whole rural India to US-Market) in 2014

[22] https://www.bcgperspectives.com/content/articles/center-consumer-customer-insight-marketing-changing-connected-consumer-india/
[23] Road to Smart Villages: An Open Innovation Approach, Berkeley Haas School of Innovation, University of California
[24] https://www.usatoday.com/story/news/world/2013/06/13/un-world-population-81-billion-2025/2420989/

Appendix

[25] The World Bank, http://data.worldbank.org/?locations=8S-IN

[26] David Wijeratne, Gagan Oberoi, and Shashank Tripathi. The New Ways to Win in Emerging Markets (2017), Strategy + Business, PWC 2017. https://www.strategy-business.com/article/The-New-Ways-to-Win-in-Emerging-Markets?gko=7f566

[27] Ibid.

[28] Ibid.

[29] 2016 report from KMPG and the Organization of Pharmaceutical Producers in India (OPPI), summarized in business-standard, http://www.business-standard.com/article/current-affairs/80-of-indian-doctors-located-in-urban-areas-serving-28-of-populace-report-116081900640_1.html

[30] Teece, David; Pisano, Gary; Shuen, Amy (August 1997). "Dynamic Capabilities and Strategic Management". Strategic Management Journal. 18 (7): 509–533.

[31] Emden, Z., Calantone, R. J. and Droge, C. (2006), Collaborating for New Product Development: Selecting the Partner with Maximum Potential to Create Value. Journal of Product Innovation Management, 23: 330–341.

[32] Henry Chesbrough; Kevin Schwartz, INNOVATING BUSINESS MODELS WITH CO-DEVELOPMENT PARTNERSHIPS, Research Technology Management; Jan/Feb 2007; 50, 1; ABI/INFORM Global, pg. 55

[33] Lee, S.M., Olson, D.L. and Trimi, S., 2012. Co-innovation: convergenomics, collaboration, and co-creation for organizational values. Management Decision, 50(5), pp.817-831.

[34] Minimal Viable Product (MVP) is a product with just enough features to satisfy early customers, and to provide feedback for future product development. Ries, Eric (August 3, 2009). "Minimum Viable Product: a guide", http://www.startuplessonslearned.com/2009/08/minimum-viable-product-guide.html

[35] See Eric Ries, The Lean Startup, 2011, for an introduction to this approach in the context of high technology startup companies.

[36] Henry Chesbrough; Kevin Schwartz, INNOVATING BUSINESS MODELS WITH CO-DEVELOPMENT PARTNERSHIPS, Research Technology Management; Jan/Feb 2007; 50, 1; ABI/INFORM Global, pg. 55

[37] Ibid.

[38] Slowinski, G. and Sagal, M.W., 2010. Good practices in open innovation. Research-Technology Management, 53(5), pp.38-45.

[39] World Economic Forum 2015, Collaborative Innovation, Transforming Business, Driving Growth

[40] Henry Chesbrough; Kevin Schwartz, INNOVATING BUSINESS MODELS WITH CO-DEVELOPMENT PARTNERSHIPS, Research Technology Management; Jan/Feb 2007; 50, 1; ABI/INFORM Global, pg. 59

[41] Österwalder, A., & Pigneur, Y. (2010). Business model generation: A handbook for visionaries, game changers, and challengers. Hoboken, New Jersey: John Wiley & Sons Inc.

[42] See Eric Ries, The Lean Startup, 2011, for an introduction to this approach in the context of high technology startup companies. (pp. 77-78).

[43] The price of this equipment, were a household to purchase it, would be approximately 5,000 Rupees or $100.

[44] Other companies are providing other potential solutions. These two examples are not intended to represent the entire spectrum of proposed solutions, nor are they intended to represent all the companies participating.

[45] World Economic Forum 2015, Collaborative Innovation, Transforming Business, Driving Growth